POW 3267

by

Simon McIlroy

First published in Great Britain in 2008 by Knights of The Ream

ISBN 978-0-9559716-0-0

Printed by Pennington Fine Colour Ltd.

www.penningtoncolour.com

Knights of the Ream,
PO Box 3255,
South Croydon, CR2 1AH

This Book is dedicated to Ian MacKenzie, my father William McIlroy, and the crew of JB 909, 408 Squadron, RCAF

POW 3267
CONTENTS

PHOTOGRAPHS and ILLUSTRATIONS

Section 1.
1. Mac, aged 16, outside the "hen-house", Dromara
2. A Hampden Aircraft
3. Hampden Aircraft
4. A Halifax Bomber
5. Halifax Bomber
6. Ian MacKenzie, Mac's Australian pilot
7. The Regular Crew
8. The Crews' Signatures
9. Mac's Flying Log Record-April, 1043
10. Hans Karl Kamp-German pilot
11. Madam Chatelin-French Red Cross nurse
12. Block 4, Belaria, Stalag Luft 3, 1944
13. Typical Room, Stalag Luft 3
14. The "Great Escapers" who were captured and shot
15. Camp Poster "Do Not Escape"
16. V2 Rocket in Flight
17. Tracer Bullet Trails to Down a V2
18. Devastation at Farringdon Market, March 1945
19. Farringdon Market

Section 2.
20. Mac, back on the farm, May 1945
21. VIP Crew with Montgomery and a French Colonel
22. Jack Conan, Army Pilot, Austria, 1947
23. Mac, 1947
24. Ian MacKenzie's Memorial Unveiled, 1955
25. Memorial, 2006
26. Street Name Plate-Jean (Ian) MacKenzie
27. Madam Lefevre with JB 909 Propeller Blade
28. The Serial Plate of JB 909
29. Mac, Visiting Memorial, May, 2005
30. Mac with Madame Hebert, May 2005
31. Mac in French Air Base BA 112 Museum
32. Mac Reunited with Alex Ager, January, 2006

PHOTOGRAPHIC ACKNOWLEDGEMENTS

Imperial War Museum (IWM)	2,3,4,5,16,17,18,19
MacKenzie Family	6,24,27,28
USAF Academy Library	13,14
Philippe Gravez	10
Hebert Family	11
Conan Family	22
McIlroy Family	1,7,8,9,12,15,20,21,23,25,26,29,30,31,32

To any reader who knows any of the air crew personnel mentioned, or there relatives, the writer would be delighted if they would contact him via the publishers.

MAPS

ACKNOWLEDGEMENTS

This true story could not have been written without my father's input of experiences, anecdotes and personal records. He has read through this account and corrected any errors I may have made.

I am indebted to Ian MacKenzie, a cousin of the pilot, Ian Cumming MacKenzie, and Roy MacKenzie, the pilot's brother, for sending me a large quantity of information and family photographs. Monsieur Philippe Gravez, of Paris, also sent me much detailed information about the flight of 14/15th April, 1943, including Luftwaffe records and material from French archives.

Eric Hebert of Reims, grandson of Madame Chatelin, very enthusiastically provided much information and contacts, particularly on the Comete Line. He and his parents were very generous to my father and me on our visit to Reims.

Thanks must also go to historian, Jean- Pierre Husson and Jacques Pernet, both of Reims. The former constructed an excellent web-site commemorating our visit to Reims in May, 2005. The web-site is, in some ways an 'electronic' memorial to Ian MacKenzie and my father. The web site may be found by typing in reims mackenzie on Google. Jacques Pernet, an aviation historian, is the driving force behind the museum at French Air Base 112, near Reims. At the museum is an exhibit dedicated to Ian MacKenzie. A copy of my father's flying log for April, 1943 is now exhibited, with a photograph of the crew.

Both my father and I appreciated the hospitality of the Deputy Mayor of Reims, M. Roger Vache, and two members of his staff – Stephane Damien and Dominique Ingres-Dunaime. They not only made many arrangements for our visit, particularly to Ian MacKenzie's memorial, in La Neuvillette, but provided information about the memorial.

I managed to trace Alex Ager, a fellow patient in Maison Blanche in 1943, and in January 2006 had the great pleasure of re-uniting him and my father, after 62 years. I am grateful to Alex for allowing me to use notes from his diaries and informing and amusing me with his many anecdotes. I also traced Bill Lott, who was in the same POW room in Stalag Luft 111 in 1944. He was the hut 'poet'.

I acknowledge the superb web-site, worldwar2exraf. Len Smith is the webmaster and through his site I traced Alex Ager and Bill Lott. And also Barbara Tracy, the grand-daughter of Don Belyea. I strongly recommend his site for all those who have an interest in the RAF in World War 2.

My profound thanks are due to my good friend, Mike Garland, who was instrumental in my starting this project by finding the memorial to Ian MacKenzie on a web-site. A visit to Reims soon followed and I found myself on a voyage of discovery.

My thanks also to Ann Roberts who typed up the original hand written manuscript. Various drafts, amendments and alterations were produced with great efficiency. Thanks to Ian Wallace who kindly translated some French letters.

I would like to record my appreciation to Mr. Jack Wagland and Mr. Terry Maher who not only arranged to reproduce all illustrations, maps, images and photographs but also the printing and binding of this book.

To all the above people I offer my sincere thanks.

Simon McIlroy

PREFACE

Let us honour if we can/ The vertical man
Though we value none/But the horizontal one.

W H Auden

These were the lines that came to mind when I was invited to write this preface.
It is a pleasure to pay tribute to Mac, the farmer's boy from Northern Ireland who became one of the many quiet heroes of World War 2. Mac's story shows that war, despite its horrors, can have a positive effect – it calls forth unexpected depths of individual courage; it reinforces the desire for freedom; and it confirms a person's faith. These are the qualities revealed in Mac the man and in his story, "POW 3267".

No negative effects of Mac's experiences are apparent either in Mac himself or in his story. It has never been in his character to feel self-pity, complacency or resentment. Mac did not need counselling or any of today's comforts to bring him to terms with the trauma of escaping from a burning aircraft, surmounting severe injuries, and being subsequently faced with incarceration in Stalag Luft 3. He had good reason by then to be grateful to the German surgeon in whose medical care he had remained for nine months in hospital – as a POW. Mac was as sensitive to the situation of his captors as he was to the plight of all those who shared his suffering in captivity.

Soon after I met Mac and found out about his experiences, I asked him two questions. The first was, " In view of the post-war controversy over the bombing of German cities, how did you feel about the role you had played?" Mac's reply was unhesitating, "At the time, it was a job well done. We had to see it as achieving the maximum destruction possible, but it was really regrettable." Mac and his wife paid a post-war visit to Hamburg. They were able to reflect on the fact that in one night of bombing 90 per cent of the city was destroyed. The second question was, "What about all that wartime hatred?" Mac's comment was, "The time is past for hatred . . . it's a matter of Christian faith – to love your enemies and to love your neighbour as you love yourself."

The task of writing began with Mac's own massively modest and understated account: it spanned only seven pages. Mac's son, Simon, deserves praise for devotedly getting the story into its present form. He was spurred on by an advert he placed on a website, ww2exraf, which led to some helpful responses from Mac's former associates and their relatives. Simon's principal sources of information, however, were French researchers/ writers/historians and the MacKenzie family, in addition to the PRO(Public Record Office) at Kew.

In completing his own mission, Simon was struck by the enormous interest by different age groups in the part played by the RAF in World War 2. For example, three respondents were the grand-daughters of some of Mac's former fellow-prisoners. We can hope, therefore, that the final story is one to be read not only by today's readers but by generations to come.
"Lest we forget. . ." Ironically, the more we can strive to pass on Mac's example of strength of character, tolerance and positive faith, the more hopeful we can be that one day we shall have a world without wars and POWs.

Kenneth Hastings

CHAPTER 1

INTRODUCTION

This is the story about my father's experiences from 1939 to 1948 when he was aged 18 to 27. He had written, at the age of 83, an eight page account, on the mild insistence of my two sisters, myself and a number of friends. The full story is far more than eight pages. His POW 'scrap book' contains over 100 pages and flying records, showing in excess of 1500 hours.

The family were aware of very little about his wartime experiences. He seldom spoke of them; his peer group in the Armed Forces were all much the same: extremely brave and courageous but reticent to talk. Only occasionally did he show us his POW 'scrap book', flying records, and a few photos.

His particular peer group were all those brave young lads of all nationalities, who flew with Bomber Command and other Air Forces during the Second World War. Over 55000 were killed in action, many laying in unmarked graves all over Europe but commemorated on the Runnymede Memorial. A good many were shot down, as he was, and spent time in hospital and POW camps. A lucky few escaped to fight another day.

The story about my father is one of many contrasts. The contrast of a tranquil way of life, as a farmer's son in Ireland, to tension of being aircrew on an RAF bomber. From complete freedom to being a Prisoner of War, in Germany. From total fitness and safety to being shot down, seriously injured and a hospital patient for nine months in Reims, France. From a peaceful rural existence in the Irish countryside to living in Sachers Hotel, one of Vienna's finest hotels, after the war. From driving a cart horse to being chauffeur driven in Churchill's Rolls Royce in London and Himmler's Mercedes Landau in Vienna. From bachelorhood to being a married man.

He never spoke in any great depth of the undoubted privations and difficulties he had to deal with. Of the terrible hunger and mind numbing boredom of being locked up in a POW camp. Never spoke of the fear and tension of going on bomber operations in the dead of night knowing that on many a previous night, fellow crews from the squadron had been blown out of the night sky by a German night fighter or flak. He never spoke of the severe pain suffered when his jaw was fractured and his right leg broken and peppered with flak and gunshot wounds; or of his anxiety and desperate pain in Reims hospital when the German surgeon discussed whether his right leg should be removed. He never mentioned any difficulties of adjusting to post war life. After all he had been through. He just got on with it. A tough little Irishman who would not be beaten by anybody or anything.

I could go on but there is a story to tell. One of quiet gallantry.

CHAPTER 2

BACKGROUND, ENLISTMENT AND INITIAL TRAINING

My father, William McIlroy, (Mac) was born in 1921 in a farmhouse in a hamlet called Leitrim, near Dromara, County Down, in the shadows of the Mountains of Mourne. The house is still there as is the village primary school (now a private house) which had 23 pupils at the time. He had two older brothers, Robert and John and a younger sister, Edith. They remained in Ireland all their lives, as farmers.

In those days life was very difficult for many people. My father had one pair of boots and as they were too hot to wear in summer, he wore no shoes at all. That was the way for many. They had no electricity but used oil lamps. As a boy, he helped on the farm, milking the cows, collecting eggs and picking apples off the trees. As a teenager he would cycle to school and spend the bus fare his father gave him on sweets at the village shop. His world was as far as he could cycle, along the country lanes. He had been to Belfast only a few times and that was merely 12 miles away.

At the age of sixteen Mac left Lisburn Technical High School with a Matriculation School Certificate. German had been one of the languages studied. Working on the farm was not an option. It was too small to support the family and he was told by his father that "he was too clever anyway!" His primary school teacher, Miss Hunter, referred to 'Willy' as " that curly haired boy with a headful of brains" The Headmaster, Mr.Charlie Adams agreed. He enrolled on a three year correspondence course with the British Institute of Engineering Technology, London, in preparation for an examination aimed at employment in the Post Office Engineering Dept. The examination age limits were 19-23. After one year, a further two years to wait to take the exams seemed, to him, an extraordinarily long time to wait, so Mac decided to join the RAF and continue to study for these examinations, in his spare time.

He duly found himself in the Belfast Recruiting Office where he volunteered for aircrew. All aircrew were volunteers. After various tests and a medical, he was found suitable for all categories but was allotted to wireless operator/air gunner (WOP/AG) in keeping with his interest in communication engineering. Mac was told, at the interview, that he would have to wait until he was 17 before entering the RAF, as he was still too young. The Christmas of 1938 was his last, as a "civilian" for quite some time. Appendix 1 shows list of units where he served.

In January 1939 Mac found himself on the way to RAF Cardington, Bedfordshire, for drill and physical training. This was followed by a posting, as an Aircraftsman (AC) to RAF Yatesbury (Wiltshire) for training in radio communication, maintenance, and the transmission of morse code at, eventually not less than 22 words per minute. Quite a feat! In addition to morse code the wireless operators had to be proficient in the use of Q codes, all of which had to be committed to memory. The Q codes were a form of shorthand to condense a long message. For instance code QFO would be used to request immediate landing, essential if the aircraft was in a critical state or short of fuel. All RAF Stations had QDMs, which was their magnetic heading for aircraft to fly towards its destination. Essential if you were lost!

To complete the course successfully, an extremely high standard in written examinations was required, as lives were dependent on the skills of these operators. Mac completed the course on 3 September 1939.

On the very same day the intake of trainees were on their final parade at Yatesbury the Prime Minister, Neville Chamberlain announced on the loudspeaker that Britain had declared war on Germany. Germany, which had already dismembered Czechoslovakia in March,1939, a year after Hitler sent his army into Austria, tried to persuade Poland to relinquish territory without a war. The Poles refused. The British Government had signed a Treaty of Mutual Assistance with Poland on 25th August,1939 two days after the Nazi-Soviet Pact. This Pact was set up to essentially deter Western powers coming to the aid of Poland. Both the Russians and Germans assumed that they could partition Poland between them without interference. They were wrong. The German refusal to withdraw its troops from Polish territory resulted in Britain's declaration of war. My father's parade corporal made some remark, typically "you bloody wireless operators will soon have had it". The impending doom bothered them less than displeasing the corporal himself, the thought of doubling round the parade square with full kit was a great deterrent to sloppy marching.

While my father and his fellow trainees were being put into shape by the parade ground corporal at RAF Yatesbury on the day that war was declared the future Commander in Chief (C in C) of Bomber Command, Air Vice Marshall Arthur Harris was with his wife in Norfolk. He was convalescing from a duodenal ulcer. After Chamberlain's speech on the radio, Harris managed to contact Air Marshall Portal, Air Member for Personnel. He wanted a job in Bomber Command and succeeded in becoming Air Officer Commanding (AOC) for No.5 Group, based in Grantham, Lincolnshire.

Dudley Saward, in his authorised biography of 'Bomber' Harris states that "Harris' vigilance at this time was of the utmost importance to the success of bombing operations in which he concentrated on criticising, improving and revolutionising every aspect of the bomber and its application to modern warfare". He continues "probably the most important action Harris took as AOC 5 Group was the setting up of a comprehensive training organisation for aircrews, which was later to become a blueprint for the later Bomber Command Operational Training Units (OTUs) and Heavy Conversion Units (HCUs).

My father's training continued under the 'old regime' but later benefited from the methods and thoroughness of the new AOC for 5 Group. After a spot of leave, back home, he was posted to the School of Air Gunnery at Stormy Down, South Wales to complete his flying training.

At the time, all wireless operators were also trained air gunners. This was the general practice for the two engined bombers, like the Hampden and Wellington. The Hampden carried a crew of four, in the most cramped of conditions. There was a pilot, a navigator, who was also the bomb aimer, a wireless operator, who manned the upper rear gun and an air gunner. When the four engined bombers (Lancasters, Stirlings, Halifaxes) entered service, the wireless operators concentrated on communications and wearing their own S (for Signals) brevet, and their "sparks" badge on their right upper sleeve.

At Gunnery School my father and his fellow volunteers learnt the mysteries of deflection, and dismantling and re-assembling Browning .303 machine guns blindfolded. It was absolutely necessary to be able to work in the dark. They fired at targets on the ground (ground to ground) and while airborne, fired at drogues, which were sausage shaped objects, made of canvas and towed by pilots. The 'towing' pilots much preferred not to do this sort of work. Completing the course meant promotion for my father to Sergeant and then a posting to the No.2 School of Air Navigation at RAF St.Athan, South Wales, as a safety wireless operator/air gunner, not to Bomber

Command where many of his fellow students were posted.

My father's task was to provide details of their aircrafts location on training flights for navigators/ observers. He flew with a number of different pilots, in Avro Ansons which were nicknamed 'Flying Greenhouses'. They had many windows and offered fantastic visibility. The Anson was designed by Roy Chadwick, who later designed the Lancaster bomber. They were ideal training planes as all the trainees could look out of the plane. They were ideal for reconnaissance work. Apart from the pilot and my father, they usually carried two or more trainees. Quite often on a training flight, where the pilot himself was receiving additional training, the pilot would follow the instructions of the navigators and get lost, somewhere over Wales or the Irish Sea. The pilot, cursing and keeping a close eye on the fuel gauge would shout "Paddy, find out where we are, those bloody idiots have got us lost". A radio fix was taken and given to the pilot and navigators. The latter then had another exercise in dead reckoning, an activity of calculating a plot of where the aircraft has travelled since it took off. Theoretically, if an aircraft flies from a given point, on a certain course at a specific speed, it is possible to calculate its position at any time. The technique relied upon accurate flying and the ability to secure information to update the navigational plot. The latter could be obtained in three ways. Visual pinpointing from map reading, radio aids or astro. The first was the most common but more difficult at night. Radio aids, which my father used to locate the aircraft when lost consisted of taking a bearing from a combination of ground stations when put together, enabled a 'fix' of the aircraft's position to be calculated. Astro navigation relied on the use of a sextant which measured the angular distance of objects (stars) by means of reflection. It required considerable expertise and was made more difficult by a shortage of suitable instruments. And it could not be employed if you could not see the stars! On these flights, quite a lot of time was spent over water – Irish Sea and the Bristol Channel. A number of times, the aircraft was searching for submarines and on one occasion the crew located and bombed a German U-Boat. On other occasions, air gunners were trained, blasting away with Lewis guns.

Whilst training had its humorous moments, it was not without danger. There was always the possibility of being attacked and sadly there were accidents. Almost 10% of Bomber Command fatalities happened at the training stage. In my father's case, one aircraft had a forced landing at

Cheriton, Hampshire in August 1940, and the following March, his plane crash landed in Worcester (his first crash). The planes undercarriage failed to drop, but fortunately none of the crew was injured.

The No.2 School of Air Navigation remained at St Athan until the base was bombed by the Germans in October 1940. There were a number of fatalities and extensive damage was done. It re-located to the safer airfield at RAF Cranage, in Cheshire. Training flights were continued and during quiet periods my father was allowed to take over the aircraft controls. He was taught to fly straight and level courses, turn port or starboard to a fresh course without losing height, and finally to perform stall turns. These were by far the most difficult and consisted of lifting the aircraft nose until it hung on its propellers. It would then fall onto its back, go into a tail spin, or fall to either side. He was restricted to the latter, as tail spins and back flips were considered too difficult to make a safe recovery.

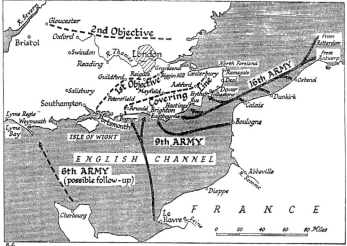

1. German Invasion Plan 1940/41

The only other major event of note during the remainder of his stay at the School was a detachment to North Weald in Essex. From here they flew a number of low level trips over the English Channel, to observe and take detailed photographs of enemy build up of personnel and defences, on or near the French coast. It is now known from captured archives that soon after war broke out, the German Admirality examined ways to invade England Operation Sea Lion. The German Admiral, Raeder, wanted entire German control of the French, Belgian, and Dutch coastlines. The capitulation of France in June, 1940 fulfilled this requirement. Hitler stated that " under certain conditions – the most important of which is achieving air superiority- a landing in England may take place" On 16th

July, Hitler issued his directive: "Since England in spite of her militarily hopeless position shows no signs of coming to terms, I have decided to prepare a landing operation against England. The preparation for the entire operation must be completed by mid-August." This task was seen as impossible by all three German services –Navy, Army and Air Force. And it remained impossible. British air power and resilience was ably demonstrated in the Battle of Britain. My father' aircraft reconnaisance operations were obviously not detected as they were never attacked. Valuable intelligence information was gathered which resulted in bombing attacks on strategic targets.

On return to Cranage, my father came across a trainee navigator with such a broad Scottish accent that he was virtually unintelligible. The Scotsman was duly sent to elocution lessons. My father's Irish accent wasn't strong enough to warrant this additional training. The Scotsman's lessons resulted in a lot of leg pulling, especially in The Three Greyhounds, the local pub in Cranage, the mess, or at local dances in Northwich, 3 miles away. It was at one of the local dances where my father met his future wife (my mother) Marjorie Worrell, a nurse at Clatterbridge Hospital, Macclesfield. He recalls "I remember going with two friends, all of us in uniform as required, to a dance in Northwich. We met nine girls there, so the numbers were right. I was the naïve country boy "claimed" by Marjorie. She, being a local Northwich girl introduced me, on later occasions to her many friends and family After a while, six of us used to meet up whenever we could. There was Vic Lorraine (wireless operator), Sam Moore (a navigator) and his wife Audrey, Pat Moore (Sam's sister), Marjorie and myself." Sam was a bit of a character. Throughout the war, he was the proud owner of a ladies bicycle, which Marjorie, as a prank, painted bright pink, much to his amusement. The opinion of his Commanding Officer is not known. Often Geoffrey Worrell, Marjorie's brother, and his friends would join the crowd. Quite a number were from the Conservative Club.

Late one evening, after a dance there was a bit of a rumpus outside the dance hall. Pat Moore was crying and Sam enquired "What's the matter?" She replied, "Vic Lorraine tried to kiss me". Readers must be reminded that this was over 65 years ago.

My father spent a fair bit of time to-ing and fro-ing between RAF Cranage and Northwich. He recalls that a number of times, Marjorie would tell him to push off and go and have a drink and play darts with Geoffrey. Quite often he would go to play snooker at the YMCA in Northwich, with 'Knocker' White, another WOP. If they had no transport, they would try to cadge a lift from cars at traffic lights. By standing on the 'rubber' in the road they got the traffic lights to change to red. They then had the cheek to ask for a lift.

Eventually, my father bought a three-wheeler red open topped Morgan, for £17. He had driven tractors on the farm, but never a car. One night, he overturned the car, cornering outside the Police Station in Holmes Chapel (Cheshire). A police sergeant came out to see what all the noise was about and found out my father had no proper documentation for the car, and no insurance. The sergeant helped to right the car and it was towed to the sergeant's house by motorbike. My father obtained some petrol and drove the car back to camp. All he got from the sergeant was a severe ticking off. Humiliating, but there was no cost or fine. Civilians generally were very proud of the RAF boys.

He must have been quite reckless as a short time after this, he drove into a ditch near a farm. The farmer towed the car out with his tractor and put the car in one of his barns. My father never drove it again and eventually the farmer bought it off him for £5. So it was back to walking and scrounging lifts!

CHAPTER 3

OPERATIONS

In April 1942, Mac attended a series of interviews and aptitude tests to assess his suitability for pilot training. These were all satisfactory but he could not take the course until completing an operational tour of 30 bombing raids. For aircraft such as Hampdens and Halifaxes, these 'tours' amounted to around 180-200 hours. A trip to Berlin could take 9 hours, one to the Ruhr industrial area, up to 6 hours. Accordingly he was posted to Bomber Command No.14 OTU - Operational Training Unit- (92 Group) at RAF Cottesmore, Rutland, to prepare for this task. The final assessments of him from RAF Cranage were summarised thus:

'A competent WOP/AG who can be relied upon at all times for fast and accurate operating. N.B. With a little more instruction this NCO should make a competent pilot'. At RAF Cranage he had received 7½ hours pilot training, on Avro Ansons.

RAF Cottesmore was equipped with Handley Page Hampdens. The aircraft has been described as follows:

It was a near perfect, if mildly eccentric, flying machine. It handled in tight turns and other off-beat manoeuvres like a fighter, the single seat cockpit cramped and cluttered though it was, provided a view from wing tip to wing tip and it was as viceless as made no matter.

Hampdens were armed with 4 Vickers guns (.303) - 2 on top of the fuselage and 2 in the belly of the aircraft. The upper gunner was also responsible for radio communications. In my father's crew there were two WOPs so they took it in turns to fly in the top position. The belly gunner had to man the guns while lying on his front, which became thoroughly uncomfortable, particularly on long trips which could be up to 9 hours. My father in common with other WOP/AGs spent a great deal of time on aircraft recognition, radio and gun maintenance.

The Hampden was nicknamed the 'Flying Panhandle' because of its long thin fuselage and was frequently confused with the German Dornier 17 and Messerschmitt 110, and there were instances of attacks, in error, by UK ground defences and fighter aircraft. In addition to gun maintenance Mac had to be capable of servicing the Vickers guns, clearing stoppages and reassembling the gun whilst blindfolded. This was necessary training as most bombing and other operations were carried out at night. Only the navigator had a light, behind his black out curtain.

My father's first training flight from Cottesmore took place on 9 May 1942. A Sgt Freeman was the pilot and it was a cross country trip, conducting QDMS and practising frequency changes on the radio equipment. For the next 3 weeks, he flew with a number of different pilots. Training trips included testing the guns, loops between beacons, (cross country exercises) weather tests and local night flying.

Other elements of training included dinghy drills, dealing with emergencies and preparing for crash landings. The latter came in rather handy for Mac. Over the next 5 years he was involved in five crash landings. There were also escape and evasion drills, invariably given by an aircrew member who had actually done it. Before every operation all aircrew members were given an 'escape kit'. This comprised of an 18" square silk map to be hidden in clothing or equipment. Also a magnetic compass, which was disguised in many ways; the most common was hidden in a collar stud. There was also a pair of plastic boxes containing concentrated food: contents included Horlicks tablets, chocolate, Benzedrine tablets for energy, malted milk and water purifying tablets. There was also a rubber water bottle holding a pint. Other items included a magnetized razor blade, fishing line and needle and thread. For operations over Germany an additional aid box was given out to provide sustenance for a total of 7 days. Information for briefing lectures on evasion was provided by M.I.9 personnel. The Second World War was the first major conflict where individuals, especially aircrew shot down, found themselves on their own deep inside enemy territory. Apart from what to do when shot down, such as avoiding capture and conduct in the event of capture, they placed great emphasis on the security of their agents and helpers. The fate of most helpers and agents who assisted an evader and were arrested by the enemy was death or torture and incarceration in a concentration camp. The capture of aircrew was invariably despatch to a POW camp. It was for this reason that aircrew were 'interrogated' to prevent infiltration into the 'escape lines' organisations. The Gestapo were making continuous efforts to do so. A trained airman was valuable. For instance, the estimated cost of training a bomber pilot was £10000. Not only was there an economic cost but according to Airey Neave "the miracle of their re-appearance at Air Force Bases and Stations in Britain has a marvellous effect on the morale of all who flew against Germany". In addition, those successful in evading capture and getting back to England provided vital information and intelligence. The whole process of training in Bomber Command resulted in an enormous number of fatalities. Throughout the war, over 5000 airmen lost their lives during training, almost 10% of all losses. Over 3000 were injured.

After 3 weeks at RAF Cottesmore, my father took part in the first 1000 bomber raid (Operation Millennium) over Germany - Cologne. Described as the greatest attack yet in aerial warfare.

Air Marshall Arthur Harris, who had been appointed C in C, Bomber Command in February 1942 had to demonstrate to the powers that be what a massive coordinated bomber force could achieve. It was expected that the sheer numbers involved would overwhelm the much improved German defences. Air Marshall Harris was appointed when Britain's fortunes were at low ebb. In the previous few months, the American Pacific Fleet was destroyed at Pearl Harbour (7th December, 1941) by the Japanese, without warning. This act brought the USA into the war. Four days later Hitler made one of his bigger mistakes by declaring war on the USA. Italy followed suit. The English speaking world were now, with a number of smaller countries such as Greece, fighting together. The Japanese had also attempted a landing on the Malayan coast and bombed Hong Kong and Singapore. Two British warships, HMS Prince of Wales and HMS Repulse had been sunk off the coast of Malaya, 2 days after Pearl Harbour. Hong Kong surrendered on Christmas Day, 1941 to the Japanese, and Rangoon, Burma was captured on 8th February 1942. One week later Singapore surrendered, 130000 allied troops becoming POWs. Three days before Harris' appointment, the Japanese bombed Darwin in northern Australia.

In the Western Desert, North Africa there were setbacks in Libya and in the Battle of the Atlantic, the success of German U-Boat patrols was beginning to strangle the maritime lifelines of critical supplies to England from the New World and Empire. Bomber Command seemed to be the only option available to strike back at the Germans. Take the war to their doorstep and beyond.

Against this gloomy backdrop, Air Marshall Harris had to contend with a number of parties with vested interests who had little or no faith in a Bomber Command offensive. They included the Army and the Admiralty who were, of course, competing for scarce resources. Harris took over as C in C when Bomber Command itself was a relatively small force. He recalls "there were only

378 aircraft serviceable with crews and only 69 of these were heavy (four engine) bombers" A Hampden bomber could carry a bomb load of 2000 lbs. a distance of about 1900 miles. A four engine Halifax bomber could carry a bomb load of 13000 lbs. a distance of about 1550 miles. It is of interest to note that the maximum bomb load a Halifax could deliver was greater than the weight of a Hampden bomber, when empty. (11800 lbs.) With these resources Harris was expected to 'punch' above Bomber Command's weight and be at the beck and call of the other services.

In addition to military pressures and demands, there were political elements to deal with. Three days after his appointment the Lord Privy Seal, Sir Stafford Cripps made a speech in the House of Commons which was considered highly damaging, not just to the morale of the RAF, but to Britain's allies, principally USA and Russia. The gist of his speech was that now the USA and Russia were involved in the conflict, the policies of Bomber Command should be changed. As a pacifist, he disliked exposing civilian populations to bombing. The truth was quite simple. Britain was fighting for her survival and civilians all over Europe had been attacked by German forces, including the Luftwaffe. As stated before, Bomber Command was the only branch of the armed forces that could strike into the heart of Germany. It would seem that for the country and Bomber Command, the appointment of Air Marshall Harris as C in C came just in time. He had to convince all the doubters that given the resources and technology, Bomber Command could deliver.

The "doubters" would not have fully appreciated at the time but the efforts of Bomber Command to date had forced the Germans to employ a significant proportion of military resources into defensive as opposed to offensive systems and equipment. For example, the number of flak guns had almost doubled, by January 1942 to 4416 heavy and 7452 medium light guns, supported by 3276 searchlights. Albert Speer, Minister for Armaments and Munitions noted that Bomber Command air raids "carried the war into our midst" "The air war opened a second front long before the main invasion in June, 1944. This comment more than validates the strategy that Air Marshall Harris was implementing. Speer notes that the increase in production of flak guns could have been employed on the Russian front, in an offensive capacity. The personnel manning the batteries and searchlights, numbering hundreds of thousands, could have been employed in other theatres of the war. Speer also notes that one third of the optical industry was engaged in producing gun sights for the batteries, and other defensive equipment. And so on.

The first 1000 Bomber Raid (30 May, 1942) which for hundreds of aircrew, including my father, was their first operation, comprised of 1047 aircraft. The force consisted of:

No.1 Group	156 Wellingtons
No.3 Group	134 Wellingtons, 88 Stirlings
No.4 Group	131 Halifaxes, 9 Wellingtons, 7 Whitleys
No.5 Group	73 Lancasters, 46 Manchesters, 34 Hampdens
91 Group (OTU)	236 Wellingtons, 21 Whitleys
92 Group (OTU)	63 Wellingtons, 45 Hampdens
Flying Command	4 Wellingtons

Appendix 2 lists all the operations my father flew on.

To prepare for a bomber offensive required a lot of planning, thought and hard work. The 'soft' requirements of planning route to target, assessing intelligence and weather reports and 'hard' requirements of preparing aircraft - maintenance, fuelling, arming guns, loading bombs.

All targets to be attacked that very night, and other nights, were decided by the War Cabinet. They determined the direction of the Air Offensive. The job of Air Marshall Harris was to implement their directives. Details of operations for that night were passed down to each of the six Bomber Command Groups. Each Group Headquarters then determined which of their squadrons would participate that night to fulfil the Group's part in the planned operations.

Orders were generally received by Squadrons during late morning.

Often an operation would be scrubbed (cancelled) even up to the point of take-off. Bad weather was often a cause. Bombs had to be removed from aircraft, returned to the dump, petrol tanks drained. The next operation could require different types of bombs and more or less petrol.

Aircrew were issued with Benzedrine tablets (wakey wakey pills) to keep them awake. A cancelled raid would inevitably mean little or no sleep.

On 'receipt' of orders the Station Commander would summon their Squadron Commanders and Operations Officer to relay the orders passed down to them. These meetings were frequently known as 'prayer' meetings.

The Operations Officer would calculate fuel requirements for their squadron(s). These requirements were based on the anticipated routes to the given target area by the Senior Navigation Officer. Routes would not always be direct to target. Account was taken not only of weather conditions, as forecast by the meteorological (met) officer, but more importantly, the location and intensity of German defence flak batteries and fighter cover. Berlin and targets in the Ruhr industrial area ('Happy Valley') were particularly well defended. The PFF (Pathfinder Force) would not only drop flares over the target but over map positions, where a 'dog-leg' route was necessary, to guide the bomber stream.

Some of the 'experienced' crews, or gen men would find out the fuel loadings for those nights operations and have a guess at that night's likely target. After aircraft were fuelled, the bomb dump personnel would get to work, loading the various types of bombs and incendiaries, and ammunition. A lot of fuel and a light bomb load indicated a deep penetration into Germany.

The crews themselves would invariably, after breakfast go to their own departments. In my father's case, it was to the wireless operators and/or gunners department. Each department had the battle order on a notice board. If you were on it, the crew would do an inspection of their part of the aircraft. Gunners would check the turrets, WOPs, the radio equipment, and so on. The target would not be disclosed until later. After lunch, the crew would try to get some sleep. Very difficult thing to do, as the tension gradually builds up. For some this trip could be their first and last trip. Mac never spoke of any fear or tension before going on an operation. He must have kept it to himself. When I asked him about it he replied "we were all young, it was exciting and we had a job to do" He did not elaborate further.

The final briefing would take place around four or five o'clock. When all duty aircrew, kitted out in flying gear, were inside the briefing rooms, doors were locked and guarded by the RAF Police. Security was and had to be tight. All windows were sealed and blacked out. Outside, even the station phone box was padlocked. In the room, the end wall was covered by a curtain. The Squadron Commander would enter the room, and in business like fashion, open the curtains to reveal a large map with the night's target clearly highlighted with a red spot.

The room would start to fug up with the smoke from up to 150 cigarettes and the odd pipe. Loud whispers would be heard, giving the opinions on whether the target was 'hard' or 'easy'. Berlin was 'hard' because of the prospect of an eight to nine hour flight and a guaranteed warm reception over the target. Ruhr Valley targets took around five hours, again with a warm reception. A number of French targets, and some in Italy were considered easier. Trips to Italy, by some 'waggish' crews did not justify a 'bomb tattoo' on their aircraft nose to signify a mission. Instead, there was an ice cream cone.

On the map there was a weather chart showing not only rain patterns and cloud formations, but wind patterns and speeds. Now knowing the target, the assembled crews would be addressed by the Senior Navigational Officer who would outline the expected route with a strand of wool or cotton, emphasizing the turning points to get over the target. The safest options were taken for minimum exposure to night fighters, flak batteries and searchlights. Navigators were given their route in the most detailed way. The final instructions, given before "any questions" was take-off time, any rendezvous that was necessary, and ETA over target. A senior officer, usually a Wing Commander would appear, reassure the crews that all information and instructions would ensure a successful and safe mission. After inviting 'any questions' he would inform crews what time to report to their 'flights', and wish the usual good luck. After that, the crews would file past a table in the room to collect escape kit, put personal items in a bag, leave a 'last letter home' if you had one, and file out.

There would now be a few hours to fill before take off. This would certainly include a crew meeting in which the pilot would brief his members. And the pre-flight meal of bacon and eggs, described as standard fare. Few civilians got hold of bacon and eggs. As a farmer's son, my father had as many eggs as he liked. Some crews also got baked beans, which was perfectly acceptable to the rest of the crew if you were the rear gunner. After the meal, the crew would collect their parachutes and other bits of flying kit and get on the transport for their aircraft at dispersal. A walk round the plane, final cigarette and get in for the off.

At OTU, RAF Cottesmore there was surprise that crews under training were part of the 1000 Bomber Raid. In essence, without the inclusion of OTUs, there would not have been such a raid. My father's flying log, for that first raid on Cologne records the following:

Took off at 11.59, Sqn Ldr Barnard was the pilot. (He was the rear gunner and W/T Operator). Bombs were dropped on target from 12,000ft. Large fires were started over the whole city. Flak and searchlights over target, Aachen and Antwerp. Trip was a great success. Flying time 4 hours 45 minutes.

Why was Cologne selected for the first 1000 bomber raid? Developments in navigational aids, especially TR.1335 (known as GEE) enabled a navigator to determine the exact position of his aircraft within a range of 350-400 miles from his base in England. The aircraft could maintain, continue along and stay on the planned flight path to target, and over it. This positional accuracy enabled higher concentration of bombers to and over target. The concentration "yardstick" in time over target was about 100 aircraft per hour. With aircraft fitted with GEE, an estimated 500 aircraft could be concentrated into a one hour raid.

Towards the end of March, Cologne was the chosen target for an experiment in concentration. An attack by 120 aircraft was concentrated in 20 minutes. The raid was a complete success. Hamburg was an alternative target for the first 1000 plane raid, but Cologne was finally selected by Harris as it was well within the GEE range and the weather was favourable.

My father said the trip was a great success. The whole raid was considered an outstanding success and time over target was an hour and a half. This stunning effort was achieved with a loss rate of 3.8% and over a third of total aircraft came from OTUs.

This massive raid completely destroyed over 6500 acres of built up area and over 250 factories were flattened or badly damaged. Energy plants, transport and communication networks were all affected. Apart from the physical damage and disruption, the raid had a huge psychological effect. Cologne was in chaos. The cage of the German High Command was well and truly rattled. There was disbelief that such a raid could be mounted.

Two days later, father took part, in the same capacity, and with the same pilot, in the second 1000 Bomber Raid, over Essen. His log records:

Took off at 11.59. High explosives and incendiary bombs dropped over target from 10,500 ft, at 0105 hours. Very heavy and accurate flak experienced. Saw an aircraft shot down over target and another before reaching target. Flying time 4 hours 45 minutes.

My father made no comment on the success of this trip. Essen was considered a very difficult target. The weather over target was invariably unpredictable and being in the heart of the industrial Ruhr, pollution made the city difficult to identify, or at least the prescribed areas. The main target area was the Krupps armaments factories. The damage inflicted on Essen by the raid was considered a partial failure. Improvements were required in navigational aids (which were under development, such as H2S and OBOE) to pinpoint targets more accurately. What the raid did however was to demonstrate to Germany that the first raid wasn't a one off. Bomber command was building up its capability.

The following three weeks reverted to 'training'. One trip was flying over the 'Wash' air firing 900 rounds from the rear turret of the Hampden. Training included using a Cine gun. This innovation was introduced by Harris, harnessing the talents of the cine-photography industry. Its present day equivalent is the flight simulator. Training by this method was initially for pilots and gunners but later extended to navigators. As described by Dudley Saward, the gunner "would be seated in a fuselage, in a suitable building. He would have all the normal equipment and controls realistically to hand as in an actual aircraft. A cinema film would be projected on a screen showing the complete development of an attack by an enemy aircraft. Attached to the pupil's gun would be a second cine projector arranged so as to superimpose on the film the flight of tracer from his guns. The pupil's gunsight would also be harmonised with a dual control set of sights in front of the instructor, who could then follow exactly what the pupil was doing and explain and correct his errors".

The third 1000 Bomber Raid, and my father's third operation took place over Bremen, flying with Flying Officer Clarke. They were, on this trip, intercepted by an ME110, a German night fighter, but got back to base in one piece. Flying time 6 hours 5 minutes, having taken off at 23.15 on 25 June, 1942.

After 11 weeks at OTU, RAF Cottesmore, my father was posted to 408 Sqn RCAF, at RAF Balderton. While he flew a number of operations, as WOP/Air Gunner, with different pilots it was on this squadron that he 'crewed up' with Sgt Ian MacKenzie. The process of crewing up was, in theory, chaotic. In practice, it was the best way. With all categories of aircrew in one large room, each category, navigators, gunners and so on would tend to remain together, drinking beer, talking shop or what they did the previous night. A pilot (skipper) would wander around the room, selecting his crew members, asking the innocent question "Are you crewed up?" Each man would size up the other. Personal chemistry was important in the team building exercise. Lives depended on it. Ian MacKenzie asked my father to join his crew, and asking if he knew any navigators looking to join a crew. Even though 408 Squadron was Canadian, there were many different nationalities. Ian was an Australian Sergeant Pilot from Brisbane. Tiny (the tallest crew member) Playfair was a navigator from Essex. He was the old man of the crew, aged 31 years. Con O'Connell, another WOP/AG was also Australian. As a crew, they took part not just on bombing raids. My father's 7th operation was 'nickelling' (leaflet dropping) over Rennes, France. These particular missions attracted a lot of criticism, as trained crews were being put at risk. However, the leaflets dropped had various themes and messages. Some were fake Nazi clothing and ration cards, designed and intended to de-stabilize the regime. Others were news sheets, dropped in occupied countries to 'maintain' the belief in allied victory and increase the ever growing spirit of resistance.

Another type of operation was mine laying. My father's 8th trip was mine laying in the Friesian Islands, off the Dutch/German coast, on 9 August 1942. Code named "Gardening", the aircraft crew had to lay a mine in a very specific location (of which there were 128). All the locations, where the crew would 'plant a vegetable', were given the names of flowers, vegetables or fruit. In the Friesian Islands my father's crew planted 'nectarines'. Each mine laying aircraft carried a single 1500lb mine, released with a drogue parachute to slow them down before they hit the water. At the time, the Battle of the Atlantic was creating, through U-Boat operations, a severe crisis. From the 7th December, 1941 to 31st July, 1942, 3.25 million tons of merchant shipping were sunk, of which 35% were British. From the 1st August,1942 to 21st May,1943 over 3.75 million tons of merchant shipping were sunk, of which over 52% were British. The Admirality demanded of RAF Coastal Command to increase patrols, principally in the Atlantic, to stem and reverse these massive losses by searching for and destroying submarines and enemy shipping. In turn RAF Coastal Command requested resources from Bomber Command to assist in this task. This reduced Bomber Command's effective offensive capacity. Harris likened the patrols as "searching for the needle in a haystack" In his view dropping mines in the main shipping lanes, particularly the Baltic Sea, and bombing ports and construction yards had and would do more damage with fewer resources employed. There was a better economic return on capital and effort. Harris quotes "mine laying put a large part of the German navy on the work of minesweeping and many workers on the repair of ships". He also warned the Admirality that they "would be the first to feel, and feel grimly, any dimunition of these efforts". He continued "they would regret the results of misemploying aircraft on the profitless task of overseas reconnaissance away from our shipping lanes".

Air laid mines had already proved their worth. Hitler's obsession that Britain was going to invade Northern Norway, which he described "is the zone of destiny in this war" resulted in concentrating all available surface ships and submarines in Norwegian waters. The 'Tirpitz' reputedly the worlds strongest battleship, was ordered to Trondheim (in January,1942) and on the 12th February Hitler ordered the 'Scharnhorst' and 'Gniesenau' to make a break from their 12 month blockade in Brest and return to the Baltic. The audacious break and "successful" voyage through the English Channel outraged the British public, and embarrassed the Government. However, what could not be made public at the time was that both vessels were damaged by mines. The 'Gniesenau' never sailed again in the war and it took 6 months to make the 'Scharnhorst' seaworthy again.

The 'Tirpitz' at the request of the Navy was sunk in Tromso Fjord, in Norway, later in the war, on 12th November 1944 by 29 Lancaster Bombers from 617 Squadron (of Dambusters fame) and 9 Squadron from No 5 Group. The specially fitted Lancasters dropped 12000 pound Tallboy Bombs, a Barnes Wallis innovation. Three bombs hit the 'Tirpitz', where she capsized at her moorings. Over half her 1900 crew perished, for the loss of one bomber, whose crew survived.

Factories inside Germany, making components for U-Boats, such as the diesel engine plants of MAN in Augsburg were also attacked. And the U-Boat pens in the Western Bases, such as Lorient and St.Nazaire in France. My father's 9th trip and his pilot, Ian MacKenzie's 4th trip on the 11th August, 1942 was a bombing mission to Le Havre. As Ian MacKenzie noted in his flying log "Bang On".

Not all trips were "bang on". My father flew with another crew on a raid to Hamburg. The combat report as follows:

Hampden "G" A.T. 182

This Hampden while leaving Hamburg at position 25 miles N.Wytenburg, time 0225, height 11000 ft. observed a twin engined enemy aircraft which was believed to be a ME 110 coming in on the Port Bow, below, about 400 yards away.

The Hampden took evasive action by turning sharply to Port and diving at the same time. This action allowed the gunners in the rear to fire a burst at the enemy aircraft who did not return the fire and broke away 600 yards astern and was not seen again.

There was bright moon with 3/10ths cloud at 5000 ft.

After the short combat it was observed that the searchlights on the ground seemed to be used to point the track of the bomber. Further evasive action being taken and no further trouble was experienced.

CREW: Pilot   Sgt. Ross

        Navigator   Sgt. Knight

        Wop/Ag   Sgt. McIlroy

Wop/Ag   Sgt. Ledoux

Combat reports, No 408 Sqdn (PRO (AIR 50/249)

My father noted in his flying log that the aircraft had been hit in 28 places with flak.

During August 1942, 408 Squadron lost a lot of aircraft, and many more had suffered a great deal of damage from German ground gunners. The Hampden ceiling, with a full bomb load was quite low compared to that of a Lancaster or Halifax, and as my father notes: "We presented a nice low target for the ground gunners. We were also sitting targets from bombs being dropped from the heavy four engined aircraft, thousands of feet above us". This prompted a decision to re-equip 408 Squadron with Halifaxes. One of the last few trips my father flew in a Hampden (and his squadron) was a raid on Kassel (27th August) about 140 miles east of the Ruhr. Churchill had received a report from Sir Stafford Cripps,around the 18th June, on a meeting he had had with a Swiss bank manager called Nussbaumer (from Schweizerischer Bankverin). In essence the report supported Harris' strategy that Bomber Command should build up its capability and not be side tracked by the demands of others, notably the Admirality and Coastal Command, whether for home or overseas operations.

Mr.Nussbaumer had highlighted four areas of difficulty for the Germans, of which one was transport. He stated that the Germans were short of 15000 locomotives and 250000 waggons, giving reasons for his observations. To aggravate the Germans difficulties, he strongly suggested bombing the Henschel works at Kassel, where 10% of German locomotive manufacturing was undertaken.

His report referred to other matters, principally that there was a real fear in Germany about Bomber Command activities. Factories producing war materials and equipment, in finished or component parts were being attacked with increasing severity and in addition many workers were being killed or made homeless. He stated that morale was very low and referred to the effectiveness of the 1000 Bomber raid on Cologne, recommending that "every effort be made to completely destroy towns and cities rather than just damage them". 408 squadron did their bit.

 408 Squadron had the dubious honour of flying on the last operation in Hampdens on 14/15 September 1942 on a bombing mission over Wilhelmshaven. My father's last trip in a Hampden

was on 7 September, to Frankfurt with Ian MacKenzie as pilot, Tiny Playfair as navigator and Con O'Connell as WOP/AG.

The conversion to Halifax bombers involved further training at RAF Leeming, on new armaments and radio equipment.

During this period my father attended a gunnery leaders course (at RAF Sutton Bridge in Lincolnshire) and was promoted to Pilot Officer. His crew at RAF Leeming, on the Halifax, now numbered seven. Ian MacKenzie was the skipper and they were joined by a flight engineer, Sgt. Lloyd McKenzie, and P/O Rod Ball WOP/AG, both Canadians, and Thomas Coupland an English bomb aimer. Two Australians, two Canadians and three English/Irish. This seven man crew more or less stayed together for all operations from RAF Leeming. After nearly 4 months of training converting to the Halifax, their first raid in the 'heavy' was on the 15th January 1943 bombing the submarine pens at Lorient. Targets included Hamburg, Cologne, Nuremburg, Berlin, Duisburg, Essen, some on several occasions. On the 1st January, 408 Sqn became part of the newly formed No 6 Group (RCAF). Their operational debut was over Essen on 3/4th January.

As the writer of this book I cannot ever accurately convey or describe the real horror of wartime bomber operations, I never experienced them. The reader of this story must imagine the freezing cold temperatures in an uninsulated aircraft for up to 9 hours. The continuous noise of the four engines, from which aircrew often experienced deafness (eg 'Lancaster Ear'), the cramped and cold conditions in a gun turret, up to 9 hours total isolation for the rear gunner, the smell of fuel oil, the utter terror of facing attack by German fighters, coned by searchlights, targeted by flak batteries. The only too real possibility of being killed, seriously injured, shot down, murdered by the German population, or becoming a POW. The pre-flight meal of bacon and eggs, for many, was literally their last meal. The mental pressure of facing these dangers and conditions, at such a young age turned boys at OTU into men on transfer to operational squadrons. It is no wonder that the mess on the station was not as formal as peacetime. New 'sprog' crews would mix with the 'gen' crews, those who had experienced operations and had survived to date. Experienced squadron colleagues did not return, leaving behind an empty bed to be filled by new aircrew the next day. My father notes some of the extraordinary things that went on in the mess. Furniture would be piled up and aircrew took it in turns to fling themselves over it, often sustaining injury. Then there was 'follow my leader' where all the members would jump through windows following the leader, return through doors, be hoisted up to print footmarks on the ceiling. Rank held no privilege. All were involved. A blind eye was 'mostly' turned to the 'Bomber Boys' antics and shenanigans. Some wouldn't be around the following week. Letting off steam was the safety valve which enabled them to face the approaching   horrors.

My father's 17th operation, in a Halifax, took place on 15 February 1943, over Cologne. To give some details of this operation the following is a combat report, after leaving the target.

While on operations to Cologne on the night of 14th/15th February,1943 P/O McIlroy the Mid-Upper Gunner of Halifax DT 769 "J" of 408 squadron sighted an enemy aircraft after leaving target, position 5110 N, 0545 E, the aircraft was first sighted on the port bow level,at 1000 yards he identified it as a JU 88. The time was 2055 hours. The visibility was very good, with a bright moon on the port side and a good background of 10/10th cloud below at 8000 feet. The Halifax was flying at 14000 feet on a course of 291 M with a true airspeed of 205 m.p.h.

The JU 88 moved from the port bow level to the port beam level and positioned himself for a beam attack at 800 yards. As the enemy aircraft came in to attack at a range of 600 yards P/O McIlroy gave the order turn port which cramped the enemy aircraft curve of pursuit and he was unable to allow enough deflection to fire at the Halifax. The Mid upper and Rear Gunner P/O Ball both opened fire at the JU 88 two bursts approximately 50 rounds per burst. The enemy aircraft broke away at 200 yards dead astern and flew in an opposite direction. After straightening up and getting back on course P/O McIlroy again sighted the same or possibly another JU 88 on the port quarter up at 800 yards. The position, course and airspeed were the same as before, time was 2100 hours. He opened fire at 600 yards and gave the order to turn 'port and climb' firing two bursts of 100 rounds. The enemy aircraft broke away at 300 yards and once again flew away dead astern in an opposite direction.

As the Halifax once again got onto course, the Mid upper sighted the JU 88 on the starboard beam, down at a range of 1500 yards, the time was now 2105 hours and the height of the Halifax was 14000 feet. The enemy aircraft positioned himself for attack on the starboard beam level at 1000 yards he came straight into attack, and at 600 yards the Halifax took evasive action by turning to starboard and the enemy aircraft opened fire with two cannons, firing from the nose. His aim was very inaccurate due to the evasive action taken by the bomber and once again the curve of pursuit was cramped. P/O McIlroy and P/O Ball both opened fire at 400 yards and continued firing until enemy aircraft broke away dead astern at 100 yards approximately, 500 rounds each. Tracer was seen to enter the JU 88 cockpit and fuselage and it is claimed as a 'probable' as it was last seen diving steeply into the cloud at 8000 feet on the port quarter below.

At 2115 hours P/O McIlroy sighted another JU 88 on the starboard bow level at 1000 yards, the enemy aircraft came straight in to attack and the Mid upper gunner gave the evasive action "turn starboard and dive". No one opened fire and the fighter broke away at 50 yards on starboard bow passing underneath the bomber to the port quarter, level, at 1000 yards on the fine port quarter the JU 88 turned round and made an approach to 700 yards, then turned and flew away dead astern in an opposite direction. The bomber did not take evasive action although the pilot was prepared for a 'Corkscrew'

There was no searchlight activity for those attacks and nothing unusual in the way of lights or illuminating shells were seen.

The pilot and crew spoke very highly of the Gunners during these attacks especially of their acute night vision.

P/O Ball the rear Gunner was trained at No.2 B & G School, Mossbank and No.7 AGS, Stormy Down.

P/O McIlroy the Mid upper was trained at G School Porthcawl, 14 OTU Cottesmore and No.46 Gunnery Leaders Course at CGS Sutton Bridge.

The manoeuvres for a 'corkscrew' is as shown

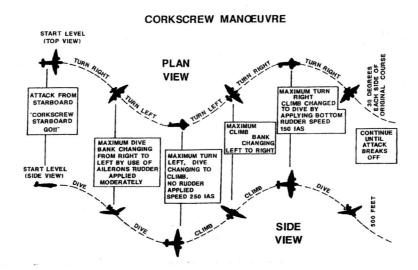

On the same raid his Australian room mate, Derek Giblin and his crew had a close shave on returning from Cologne to Leeming. While preparing to land, the port outer engine burst into flames and the port inner lost power. The pilot F/L Boosey managed to gain 100ft and five of the crew baled out before the Halifax crash landed. The pilot also managed to evacuate, but one crew member, F/O Parker, lost his life. His parachute had not fully deployed.

Cologne was re-visited again later in the month. From my father's notes the more raids the MacKenzie crew went on, the more it seemed that the flak and searchlights became more intensive and increasingly accurate. They were hit on a raid over Berlin (27/3/43). The port outer engine caught fire over the target but the pilot managed to fly the aircraft back on 3 engines. This trip was my father's 24th and there was a feeling that luck was maybe running out. 1943 was a particularly bad year for Bomber Command during which a massive one third of all crews and aircraft lost during the war were sustained. The so-called 'Battle of the Ruhr' had begun. On hearing of the target in the briefing room, the feeling, quoting Don Charlwood, was that we were "men before a firing squad of erratic marksmen".

By the end of February,1943 Harris had not only his 'management' team in place but almost 1000 front line bombers of which 2/3 were four engined "heavies". This, of course, included the Halifaxes of 408 Squadron (Goose) RCAF which was now part of No 6 Group, RCAF.

The majority of the bombers were now able to operate with new navigational aids, H2S and Oboe and new bomb aiming aids. This enabled them to fly to and over target in poor weather conditions and moonless nights. The increased accuracy of pinpointing targets, identified and target marked by the Pathfinder Force, and the greater bomb loads carried resulted in greater devastation. The 'Battle of the Ruhr' opening offensive started with an attack on Essen on the 5/6th March. The aiming point was the centre of the Krupps armaments factories.

My father's crew flew on the 2nd attack on Essen, but returned early with engine trouble. Before his next attack on Essen, they took part in a raid to Duisburg (26th March) It was the first occasion that the Germans used decoy flares, a successful tactic as almost a quarter of the aircraft bombed them. The resulting fires were also bombed by aircraft following later in the bombing stream. Skymarking techniques had to change to ensure that enemy decoy flares did not interfere with the success of the raids.

My father's last three trips were, in his words 'all disasters'. On the 3 April 1943, after bombing Essen, they crash landed back at base, undercarriage up, destroying the aircraft. The crew report as follows:

Took off at 19.51, landed 2.07. Good visibility in target area, with slight ground haze. The target was identified by PFF markers. A pinpoint was obtained on the primary and an attack was made from 18,000ft at 22.02 on a heading 180° N. Green markers were in bomb sight at moment of release but no results were observed, but it is sure that bombs fell in the target area. The fires in the target area seemed to be well started and these were visible from 70 miles away. On return to base, the undercarriage of this plane would not come down so the pilot F/Sgt Wood was compelled to make a belly landing. The landing was made OK and none of the crew were injured. It is not yet known why this undercarriage would not come down.

Load carried

2 x 1000lb

630 x 4lb

48 x 30lb incendiaries

The ORB (Operations Record Book) stated the following: Weather fair to cloudy, with good visibility.

We were called upon for a full effort and 12 aircraft were prepared for operations. All aircraft were off on time and 9 were successful in attacking the target area, same being Essen. One aircraft returned to base early owing to the illness of the pilot. Two aircraft failed to return from this operation.

By the end of April, Essen had suffered 4 major attacks. After the third attack Goebells visited what was left of the city on 10th April. He noted in his diary:

We arrived in Essen before 7am. Deputy Gauleiter (District Leader) Schlessman and a large staff called for us at the railway station. We went to the hotel on foot because driving is quite impossible in many parts of Essen. The walk enabled us to make a first hand estimate of the damage inflicted by the last three raids. It is colossal and indeed ghastly. This city must, for the most part, be written off completely. The city's building experts estimate that it will take 12 years to repair the damage. Nobody can tell how Krupps can go on. Everyone wants to avoid transplanting Krupps from Essen. There would be no purpose in doing so, for the moment Essen is no longer an industrial centre the English will pounce upon the next city, Bochum, Dortmund or Dusseldorf.

Two days after Goebbels made his diary entry, Stalin signalled Churchill, welcoming the bombing of Essen, Berlin and other industrial centres of Germany.

On the 8th April, after an operation over Duisburg, my father's plane crash landed at RAF Burn, undercarriage down. This was his third air crash. Luck really was running out. The possibility of completing a full tour of 30 operations was becoming just that. A possibility only.

1. Mac, Aged 16, outside the "hen-house", Dromara

2. A Hampden Aircraft   IWM CH 3478

3. Hampden Aircraft   IWM HU 95902

4. A Halifax Bomber   IWM CH 6615

5. Halifax Bomber   IWM HU 95901

6. Ian MacKenzie, Mac's Australian pilot

7. The Regular Crew
From Left to Right: McIlroy, Coupland, Ball, MacKenzie,
O'Connell, Playfair, McKenzie
MOTTO: Hold Tight! Here I Come!

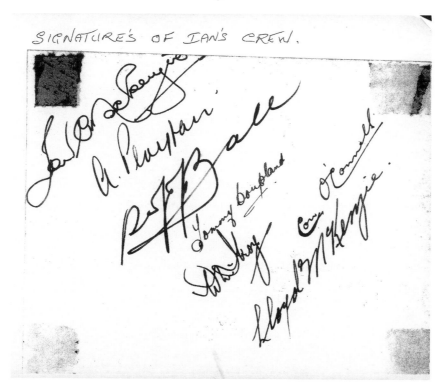

8. The Crews' Signatures

APRIL 1943

						HRS	MIS
					Time carried forward :—	1167.40	203.50

Date	Hour	Aircraft Type and No.	Pilot	Duty	REMARKS (Including results of bombing, gunnery, exercises, etc.)	Flying Times Day	Night
3.4.43	1950	DT673(G)	F/Sgt WOOD	REAR GUNNER AND W/T OPERATOR	25 OPS ESSEN + BOMBING. [CRASH LANDED AT BASE - U/C UP]	✓ ✓	6.20
8.4.43	2200	B65u (L) JB909	F/Sgt BLACKHALL	REAR GUNNER W/T OPERATOR	26 OPS DUISBURG - BOMBING (CRASH LANDED AT RAF BURN - U/C DOWN.)	✓	5.00
14.4.43	2150	DT673(G)	P/o MacKenzie..	REAR GUNNER W/T OPERATOR	27 OPS STUTTGART - BOMBING.	6.00 MISSING.	

(Landed by parachute in France with severe leg and jaw wounds caused by German night Fighter - taken prisoner of war

J H Christofe
C.O. "408" Sqdn.
P 12¹

9. Mac's Flying Log Record-April 1943

Hans-Karl KAMP

Hans Karl Kamp, The German Pilot who shot down Halifax JB 909

10. Hans Karl Kamp, In a Airfield Control Room, shown second from left.

11. Madam Chatelin-French Red Cross Nurse

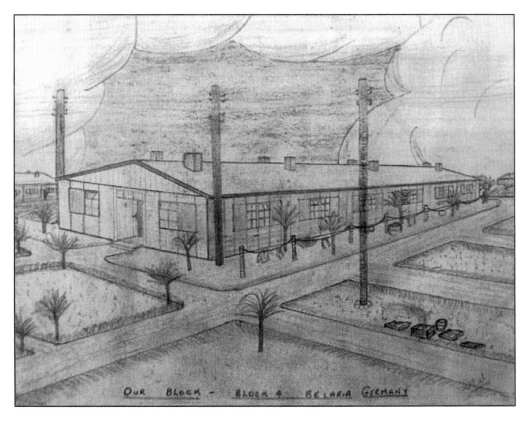

12. Block 4, Belaria, Stalag Luft 3, 1944

Typical Room, Stalag Room 3

13. Typical Kitchen Area

1. Birkland, H. 2. Brettell, E.G. 3. Bull, D. 4. Bushell, R.J. (Big X) 5. Casey, M.J.

6. Catanach, J. 7. Christiansen, A.G. 8. Cochran, D.H. 9. Cross, K.J. 10. Espelid, H.

11. Evans, B.H. 12. Fuglesang, N. 13. Gouws, J.S. 14. Grisman, W.J. 15. Gunn, A.

16. Hake, A.H. 17. Hall, C.P. 18. Hayter, A.R.H. 19. Humphreys, E. 20. Kidder, G.A.

21. Kierath, R.V. 22. Kiewnarski, A. 23. Kirby-Green 24. Kolanowski, A.W. 25. Krol, S.

14. The "Great Escapers" who were captured then shot

26. Langford, P.W. 27. Leigh, T.B. 28. Long, J.L. 29. McGarr, C.A. 30. McGill, G.E.

31. Marcinkus, R. 32. Milford, H.J. 33. Mondschein, J.T. 34. Pawluk, K. 35. Picard, H.A.

36. Pohé, P.P. 37. Scheidhauer, B.W. 38. Skantzikes, S. 39. Swain, C.D. 40. Stevens, R.

41. Stewart, R.C. 42. Stower, J.G. 43. Street, D.O. 44. Tobolski, P. 45. Valenta, E.

46. Walenn, G.W. 47. Wernham, J.C. 48. Wiley, G.W. 49. Williams, J.E. 50. Williams, J.F.

14. The "Great Escapers" who were captured then shot, on the direct orders of
Adolf Hitler

To all Prisoners of War!

The escape from prison camps is no longer a sport!

Germany has always kept to the Hague Convention and only punished recaptured prisoners of war with minor disciplinary punishment.

Germany will still maintain these principles of international law.

But England has besides fighting at the front in an honest manner instituted an illegal warfare in non combat zones in the form of gangster commandos, terror bandits and sabotage troops even up to the frontiers of Germany.

They say in a captured secret and confidential English military pamphlet,

THE HANDBOOK
OF MODERN IRREGULAR
WARFARE:

". . . the days when we could practise the rules of sportsmanship are over. For the time being, every soldier must be a potential gangster and must be prepared to adopt their methods whenever necessary."

"The sphere of operations should always include the enemy's own country, any occupied territory, and in certain circumstances, such neutral countries as he is using as a source of supply."

England has with these instructions opened up a non military form of gangster war!

Germany is determined to safeguard her homeland, and especially her war industry and provisional centres for the fighting fronts. Therefore it has become necessary to create strictly forbidden zones, called death zones, in which all unauthorised trespassers will be immediately shot on sight.

Escaping prisoners of war, entering such death zones, will certainly lose their lives. They are therefore in constant danger of being mistaken for enemy agents or sabotage groups.

Urgent warning is given against making future escapes!

In plain English: Stay in the camp where you will be safe! Breaking out of it is now a damned dangerous act.

The chances of preserving your life are almost nil!

All police and military guards have been given the most strict orders to shoot on sight all suspected persons.

Escaping from prison camps has ceased to be a sport!

15. Camp Poster "Do Not Escape"

16. V2 Rocket in Flight   IWM CU 4529

17. Tracer Bullet Trails to Shoot Down a V2   IWM HU 87733

18. Devastation at Farringdon Market, After a V2 Rocket Attack, March 1945
IWM HU 97015

19. Farringdon Market After the March 1945 Attack
IWM HU 97014

CHAPTER 4

SHOT DOWN

The 15th April, 1943, is a date my father will not forget. Some 462 aircraft were despatched to bomb Stuttgart, of which 370, 80%, reached the target area.

From Night Raid Report No 310, zero hour was 0046, period of attack 0045-0125 hours. At zero hour 17 Y-aircraft were to drop red T.I.s (target indicators) blindly on the aiming point and on the same heading 10 seconds later to release bundles of white flares in a stick at 5 second intervals. The Y-aircraft were to be followed, 2 minutes later, by 5 "marker illuminators" instructed to identify the aiming point visually and mark it with green TIs; if necessary they were to release flares 10 seconds after bombing and on the same heading. 19 'backers up' were to follow the "marker illuminators" and aim green TIs at the estimated centre of the area of green TIs. The last 12, who were to attack between 0057 and 0124 hours were to aim their green TIs to overshoot by a second.

The main force were to attempt to identify the aiming point, but if this proved impossible, they were to aim at the estimated centre of the area marked by previous TIs. The red TIs and illuminating flares were for the use of the PFF (Pathfinder Force) and were to be ignored by the main force.

The target area was the north of Stuttgart where most of its factories were concentrated, including manufacturers of ball bearings, precision instruments, machinery and power plants.

No 6 Group (RCAF) made ready 28 Halifaxes and 81 Wellington bombers. 10 Halifaxes were sent by 408 Sqn. The ORB (Operations Record Book) states the following:

Weather cloudy with slight rain during midday with good visibility. Ten aircraft were prepared for operations and all were off on time. The target for this operation was Stuttgart. Six aircraft were successful in attacking the primary, and all report a successful raid. One aircraft returned to base early owing to the rear turret going U/S (unserviceable) and another returned owing to sluggish condition of the motors. Two aircraft failed to return from this operation and below are the operation hours and trips of the members of the crews.

No	Name		Trips	Operational hours/mins
J14135	P/O L Usher	Pilot	2	12.35
J13820	P/O G Parkinson	Nav/B	-	-

R137824	Sgt I McDonald	Nav/B	-	-
1086282	Sgt J Courtney	WOP/AG	-	-
R105201	Sgt W Reed	AG	1	7.49
J16465	P/O Raymond	AG	-	-
R59857	Sgt R Dressler	F/Eng	-	-

For the pilot, this would have been his first trip as 'first' pilot. For 5 of his crew members it was their first operational trip. All were Canadian, except Sgt Courtney who was English. He was the only one to be killed, all other crew members becoming POWs. Very sadly, Sgt Courtney's brother, William James was also killed in the war.

My father's aircrew records as follows:-

This aircraft EQ-G JB909 took off at 21.15, failed to return and no further news has been heard from same. Below are operation hours and trips of the crew:

No	Name		Trips	Operational hours/mins
AUS405005	P/O I MacKenzie	Pilot	19	112.21
118652	F/O A Playfair	Nav/B	23	136.58
134394	Sgt T Coupland	Nav/B	12	71.31
AUS303033	P/O C O'Connell	WOP/AG	24	139.26
50572	P/O W McIlroy	WOP/AG	27	151.00
R62925	F/S J Murray	WOP/AG	19	107.20
R71002	Sgt L McKenzie	F/Eng	10	58.37
R127907	Sgt W Canter	Co/Pilot	1	7.07

Both aircraft had reached the target area. P/O Ushers plane was shot down on their return by a night fighter crashing at Montescourt-Lizerolles (Aisne) 14km south of St Quentin, France.

My father notes the following;

Our aircraft was attacked by, I believe, an FW 190 (it was in fact an ME 110) night fighter, 4km NW of Reims. Our aircraft was riddled with bullets like a colander. The plane caught fire and the skipper, P/O Ian MacKenzie ordered everyone to bail out. Ian sacrificed his life in order that the burning bomber did not come down on houses in the village of La Neuvillette, where it crashed nearby, at around 3.15am. As the rear gunner on this trip, I did not hear Ian's order to bail out. All communication systems were blasted away. I was close to the centre of the explosion and so felt the full blast of flying debris. I received severe leg and jaw injuries and numerous wounds over the rest of my body and my hearing was severely affected. I couldn't even hear the noise of the bomber's engines, something you could not fail to hear. So even if the communications systems were working properly I would not have heard any orders to bale out anyway. The paradox is that I could see and sense the pandemonium but could not hear it. I had great trouble moving my severely damaged right leg out of the turret in order to escape. And one of the four rear guns was bent upwards to add to the difficulty of getting out. (A post war X Ray showed 100 'foreign bodies' in his leg) I baled out through the rear turret which had to be manually operated in order to get out at 12000ft. Fearing that my parachute may have been damaged, I pulled the ripcord immediately. I had a painfully slow descent.

One minute noise, fire, explosions and confusion, next a strange form of tranquillity, albeit in extreme pain in moonlight. Pandemonium to silence.

The (translated) French police report from Police Commissioner Charboneau dated 15th April is as follows:

Subject: English Airplane Crash at La Neuvillette

I have the honour to advise you of the crash of an English airplane which was downed by a German fighter just outside the outskirts of Reims; I have yet to obtain the exact time, but have the following information:

At 2.55 am, an English airplane was spotted by a German searchlight, hit by a burst of machine gun fire and caught fire. After staying in the air for 7 to 8 minutes, it fell to earth at La Neuvillette, about I kilometre beyond the canal bridge and about I kilometre to the right hand side. The tail of the airplane was found about 800 metres from the canal bridge and 50 metres from the edge (of the canal itself) on the right hand side of the road to Laon.

Mr. Auzas, Police Captain arrived on the scene and made his report.

On the basis of testimonies made to this police officer by one of its wounded occupants, the crew was composed of 8 men some of whom were able to jump out by parachute.

At the time we received this information, there was a man with an injury to his thigh, discovered 2 to 300 metres before Cernay and who was taken to the White House Hospital; another about which I am unaware where he landed was taken to the same hospital by the Germans, 3 captured alive by the Germans and taken to Courcy. It was possible to see under the debris (of the airplane) a camera. I do not know what happened to the two others (i.e. crew members)

The warden of the Paix Bertrand who had been posted to La Neuvillette and was immediately taken to the site of the crash was asked to leave by the German military police.

I am unaware whether any of the machine gun bullets that fell on the town caused any injury.

The report (in French) is shown in Appendix 3

Mac's account continues:

My slow descent gave me time to think how I might land on one leg to prevent further damage to the other (right) leg. The impossibility of surviving if landing in a lake or river bothered me somewhat. Fortunately I landed in a field. Immediately I threw away my escape kit, and German marks and French francs (about £12.00 worth, issued before take off and contained in a coloured purse) as far as I could into the long grass. I was physically unable to hide or bury my parachute. Of the aircrew, the Australian pilot, Ian MacKenzie lost his life as the burning Halifax bomber crashed into the ground near La Neuvillette, Reims. Canadian Sgt.Wilf Canter, flying his second operation as the second pilot was the only member of the crew, after baling out, to evade capture. The rest of the crew were taken POW, although my father, who was seriously injured, spent nine months in Reims Hospital before being transferred to Stalag Luft III in January, 1944.

The horror and confusion of that flight is highlighted from answers to questionnaires completed by the crew members of JB 909. Canter's report was filed in June 1943 when he got back to Liverpool, England via Gibraltar. The remaining reports were completed in May 1945, when the surviving crew members returned to England.

Canter's report on the loss of JB 909 follows. Curiously my fathers name is omitted, although Canter did state, on a different report, that he only knew the name of the pilot.

MOST SECRET

Operational Research Section (B.C.)   Report No. K. 14

Report on the Loss of Halifax II No.JB 909 ("G" of No.408 Squadron) on 14/15th April, 1943 while on a bombing operation against Stuttgart

1. **Crew**

Pilot:	P/O McKenzie	(fate not known)
2nd Pilot:	Sgt. W L Canter	(interrogated) - On his 2nd trip
Navigator:	F/O A Playfair	(fate not known)
Air Bomber:	Sgt T J Coupland	.. .. ..
W/Operator:	P/O O'Connell	.. .. ..
Air Gunner:	F/Sgt J S Murray	.. .. ..
Air Gunner:	Sgt M Lloyd	.. .. ..

2. Sgt Canter was not part of the normal crew of this aircraft but was flying as 2nd Pilot to gain experience. It was his second operational trip.

3. The aircraft, from which the mid upper turret had been removed, took off from Leeming, about 10 minutes late owing to trouble with the R/T. The fault was located as due to a switch having been turned off and when this was rectified there was no further trouble with it.

4. The lost time was made up successfully and the aircraft bombed the target from 16000 feet at the time allotted to it.

5. No incident occurred until about 0330 when the aircraft was attacked by an unseen night fighter while flying at 16000 feet over Reims at a speed of about 160 I.A.S and heading 290°- 300°. It was a bright moonlight night with good visibility, and the aircraft was on the track ordered.

6. The crew were taken completely by surprise and the first warning of the attack was when the crew saw tracer coming from astern and about 20° above. The fighter only fired one burst and the next thing that happened was that the whole of the fuselage was on fire from the rest position to the tail.

7. The Mid Upper Gunner was looking through the peephole in the floor and the 2nd Pilot considers that the fighter would undoubtedly have been seen had a mid upper turret been

fitted.

8.   The 2nd Pilot believes that the two Air Gunners and the Wireless Operator were killed in this attack as no reply could be got from them on the intercom.

9.   The Flight Engineer and the 2nd Pilot tried to approach the fire to attempt to extinguish it but the heat was too much for them.

10.   The engines and controls were probably hit as the Pilot had great difficulty to manage the aircraft, but he immediately started diving and turning as far as he was able.

11.   The fire burnt fiercely but appeared to be confined to the fuselage and it was decided to abandon the aircraft, through the forward escape hatch. The Air Bomber went first, followed by the Navigator and 2nd Pilot. The latter estimates that three or four minutes had elapsed between the first burst of enemy fire and the time when he left the aircraft. He jumped feet first facing the wind and estimated the height of the aircraft to be 8-10,000 feet and it was flying straight and diving rapidly. Flight Engineer and the Pilot were preparing to abandon the aircraft when the 2nd Pilot jumped.

12.   There were no searchlights and there appeared to be no ground cooperation until the aircraft was set on fire, when it was immediately coned and held all the way to the ground.

13.   There was a slight breeze and the 2nd Pilot broke his leg on landing.

14.   After he left the aircraft the 2nd Pilot saw it turn round on a smooth circle and fly straight and level for a short period and then it suddenly dived straight into the ground, where it burnt fiercely and then seemed to explode, and the fire became scattered over a wide area.

15.   No explosion occurred in the air and the 2nd Pilot considers that there should have been sufficient time for the Flight Engineer to bale out before the aircraft dived into the ground.

16.   The next day the member of the crew interrogated saw a party of German soldiers pass his landing place, escorting two prisoners but he was not able to see whether they were members of his crew.

17.   The 2nd pilot heard from local French sources that another British aircraft was shot down by fighters in the same district, on 14/15 April and a further British aircraft on the following

night. Informant believed this to be due to fighters also, and as far as he knew it was the only British aircraft in the vicinity that night.

18. Sgt.Canter says that there is a G.A.F. Station about 1 to 2 miles N.W. of Reims. The aircraft operating from it are FW.190 and there was considerable activity of these aircraft every day. There is also another aerodrome South of Reims but he believed this to be a training establishment as the aircraft there were biplanes.

20. [sic] He also saw a large German twin-boomed aircraft fly over very fast at a low altitude. It was larger than a Lockhead Lightning but he could not recognise what it was from his recollection of German aircraft silhouettes. (It is suggested from the description that it may have been a Focke-Wulf FW 189).

21. He noticed particularly (through field glasses) that there were projecting from the nose four rods, two on each side, which terminated in 3 pronged tridents. He was unable to give an estimate of the length of the rods but it is believed from his description that they were of the order of a foot or two and that the trident ends were small compared with the length of the rods.

Questionnaires of the other crew members, some years later, are as follows:-

QUESTIONNAIRE FROM RETURNED AIRCREW

Loss of bomber aircraft

NUMBER. 50572

RANK. P/O

NAME. McIlroy W.A.

SQUADRON.408

AIRCRAFT.JB-909 EQ-G

TYPE OF AIRCRAFT. Halifax II

DATE OF LOSS. 14/15.4.1943

TARGET. Stuttgart

HOW MANY OPS.27

DUTY. Rear Gunner

DATE OF INTERROGATION. 14.5.1945

INFORMATION EXTRACTED FROM. POW report

NARRATIVE OF EVENTS FROM TAKEOFF TO LANDING.

Took off from base at Leeming to bomb Stuttgart on the night of April 14, 1943. The weather was clear and visibility was good for starlight. We reached the target safely and dropped our bombs on the PFF marking flares and set course for home. When in the vicinity of Rheims the aircraft was hit and set on fire by what seemed to be heavy flak. I was in the tail turret and did not see the flak and did not know what had actually happened, and could not ascertain as I was severely injured. A short time after this I noticed a single engine fighter 600 yards dead astern, flying at our own level. Although our aircraft was already well alight the fighter was coming closer and opened fire from a distance of 400 yards and as my turret was still serviceable, I retaliated by a long blast until eventually he broke off the attack and dived to starboard. Due to my injuries I could not leave to inspect the damage done, and as I was not in intercom with the other members of the crew I decided the aircraft was in no state to fly much longer as flames were streaming past my turret, so I abandoned by falling through the turret door, which I adjusted so that I fell to the port of the aircraft. I have no idea of what happened after as I must have lost consciousness, for when I awoke on the ground everything was peaceful and quiet and nowhere was any sign of the burning aircraft.

Informant states that in conversation with the navigator and wireless operator afterwards he learned that the whole aircraft was in flames after being hit by flak. The navigator and wireless operator should supply more precise details.

My father reconciled his account of his descent by parachute to the official account he made after he was repatriated. He remembers the painful and slow descent, and throwing his escape kit away after landing on his 'good' leg. He then lost consciousness through the pain and trauma of being shot down, as he was found and woken by a German soldier. I would imagine everyone remembers their first parachute jump. It was his first and only jump. His only recollection of parachute training at RAF Yatesbury was that, if he had to bale out of stricken aircraft, he had to count to five before pulling the D-ring (ripcord) There was no 'practical' such as jumping off a gate, and pretending.

Other crew questionnaires follow:

QUESTIONNAIRE FROM RETURNED AIRCREW

Loss of bomber aircraft

NUMBER. 118652

RANK. F/O

NAME. Playfair A.

SQUADRON.408

AIRCRAFT.JB-909 EQ-G

TYPE OF AIRCRAFT. Halifax II

DATE OF LOSS. 14/15.4.1943

TARGET. Stuttgart

HOW MANY OPS.23

DUTY. Observer

DATE OF INTERROGATION. 28.5.1945

INFORMATION EXTRACTED FROM. POW report

NARRATIVE OF EVENTS FROM TAKEOFF TO LANDING.

My aircraft set course for Stuttgart at approximately 20:00 14/15 April; 1943. The outwards journey was more or less uneventful. The weather was good. Navigation straight forward. Approaching the target we saw a number of fairly widespread fires. Made a bombing run from North to South encountering a fair amount of flak during the same. The bomb aimer identified attacking point, photo flash OK and a steady run was made. Bombs all released at line off target, I believe at approximately 01:30. On the homeward journey, pin pointed Chalons-sur-Marne, last turning point for the English coast. Moon was nearly full, clear sky. No searchlights visible, no flak flashed at all. Approximately 03:00, period of attack, between Chalons and Rheims came the attack. I was concentrating on the GEE box from which I was getting good results, when the aircraft shuddered as though caught in a terrific slipstream. A few seconds after, the pilot gave orders to crowd into the front of the aircraft as he could not keep the nose down. I moved forward against the bomb aimer, watching the ASI needle and altimeter, whose pointers were fluctuating wildly. I felt that the aircraft was repeatedly on the point of stalling. After a short time, the pilot seemed to regain control and asked "can you not get that fire out". That was the indication I had that we were on fire. I pulled my blackout curtain and looked down the aircraft and saw the fuselage was blazing badly. I have since heard from the wireless operator that the rear of the port wing was also ablaze. The pilot then gave the order to abandon the aircraft. I donned my parachute, put the GEE detonators in operation, removed the front escape hatch, advised the pilot and abandoned the aircraft. I delayed my drop and when the chute opened, turned to follow the aircraft's movements. The port side of the fuselage seemed to be blazing furiously and after continuing on course for sometime, the aircraft seemed to make a turn of approximately 180 degrees descending all the time. I estimated we were attacked at approximately 12,000 feet and the aircraft was abandoned between that height and 10,000 feet. I heard no warning of fighter attack over intercom.

QUESTIONNAIRE FROM RETURNED AIRCREW

Loss of bomber aircraft

NUMBER. 1343940

RANK. Sgt

NAME. Coupland T.J.

SQUADRON.408

AIRCRAFT.JB-909 EQ-G

TYPE OF AIRCRAFT. Halifax II

DATE OF LOSS. 14/15.4.1943

TARGET. Stuttgart

HOW MANY OPS.13

DUTY. Bomb Aimer

DATE OF INTERROGATION. 27.4.1945

INFORMATION EXTRACTED FROM. POW report

NARRATIVE OF EVENTS FROM TAKEOFF TO LANDING.

Base: Leeming, take off time approximately 19:00 hours. Weather conditions, very good, full moon. Our take off was slightly delayed by intercom trouble which was rectified before take off.

Trip to the target was uneventful. Target well alight, plenty of searchlights, flak was light and unpredicted. Homeward trip was uneventful till over Rheims we were attacked by a fighter from astern and below, fighter approached unobserved. The incident happened after the target had been bombed. The aircraft immediately set on fire and burned very fiercely, flt/engineer and mid upper gunner tried to put out the fire, but was hopeless. Ordered to bale out, aircraft on fire was coned by searchlights and held until it crashed.

QUESTIONNAIRE FROM RETURNED AIRCREW

Loss of bomber aircraft

NUMBER. 403033

RANK. F/Lt

NAME. O'Connell C.A.

SQUADRON.408

AIRCRAFT.JB-909 EQ-G

TYPE OF AIRCRAFT. Halifax II

DATE OF LOSS. 14/15.4.1943

TARGET. Stuttgart

HOW MANY OPS.24

DUTY. Wireless Operator

DATE OF INTERROGATION. 28.5.1945

INFORMATION EXTRACTED FROM. POW report

NARRATIVE OF EVENTS FROM TAKEOFF TO LANDING.

On the night of 14.4.943 I was in aircraft EQ-G based at Leeming. The target was Stuttgart. The trip was uneventful on the journey to the target. The target was bombed and course set for home. At 02:15 whilst flying at 10,000 feet the aircraft immediately jumped into the air whilst shells exploded around and in the machine. One shell burst to the rear of the wireless operator's seat, the H2S apparatus saving the life of the operator. The mid upper gunner was stationed in the engineer's dome to keep watch on the port and starboard beams. He was wounded in the upper arm and also the last two fingers on the left hand. The pilot immediately placed the aircraft in a dive, requesting the flt/engineer to stay and try to control the fire amidships. This he did, but with little apparent results. The pilot, in the meantime tried to feather the starboard inner engine, but again, no results. The intercom then failed and the pilot ordered the crew to come forward and bale out, stating that he could not control the aircraft. The baling out went according to plan with the exception of the rear gunner who not being able to get through to the front of the machine, left from the rear door. When I left the pilot was preparing to follow me. I landed by the side of the canal and found I had a small flesh wound in the right leg. This I attended to and then disposed of my parachute and harness by sinking them in the canal. Then headed in a circle of about a half a mile from the burning aircraft until I was to the West of it, then dawn was breaking. I entered a coppice and stayed there for a day.

QUESTIONNAIRE FROM RETURNED AIRCREW

Loss of bomber aircraft

NUMBER. C-92946

RANK. P/O

NAME. McKenzie L.W..

SQUADRON.408

AIRCRAFT.JB-909 EQ-G

TYPE OF AIRCRAFT. Halifax II

DATE OF LOSS. 14/15.4.1943

TARGET. Stuttgart

HOW MANY OPS.11

DUTY. Flt/engineer

DATE OF INTERROGATION. 11.5.1945

INFORMATION EXTRACTED FROM. POW report

NARRATIVE OF EVENTS FROM TAKEOFF TO LANDING.

Usual trip until a fighter attacked from underneath on the way home. There were three explosions in the fuselage and fire broke out inside and outside. No one saw the fighter. It was at Rheims in bright moonlight. When I looked for the pilot's chute, I couldn't find it and he said he knew where it was. He tried to make a forced landing. The machine stayed intact as far as I could see. The Germans claimed his body was found in the machine. We were on the way home.

Inevitably there is a certain amount of confusion of exactly what happened and the sequence. My father believed the plane was hit by flak, but there was no flak, as confirmed by other crew members. A night fighter, an ME110, approached unseen and attacked. This may well have been the same fighter my father saw and retaliated against with a "long blast".

However, an Australian newspaper article (The Sunday Mail) appearing on 15 August 1982 states that one of the surviving members of the crew spoke to Ian MacKenzie's mother after the war. It is assumed it would have been the Australian WOP Con O'Connell who told Mrs MacKenzie that Ian's Halifax was attacked by two fighter planes. It may have been the second one my father saw and opened fire on, but he was very seriously injured from the first attack. Realising the hopelessness of the situation and without being able to receive or give information to the pilot, he baled out.

What is not in doubt is that Ian MacKenzie ordered the crew to bale out, which, apart from the rear gunner, went according to plan. Ian would have been last to leave the aircraft but Con O'Connell told Mrs MacKenzie (newspaper article) that he stayed with the plane and just managed to get if over the rooftops and crashed on the outskirts of the town (La Neuvillette).

A (French) eyewitness states "when he passed in front of us, he was only a few metres from the ground. The plane was terribly damaged and by the light of the flames we could clearly see the pilot". As if in a last supreme effort he managed to miss the last houses and crashed North of the port. Despite the curfew, several men rushed to the site but the arrival of the Germans forced them to retreat.

Luftwaffe records, as shown, name German fighter pilot Staffelkapitan Hans-Karl Kamp flying a ME 110 of 7./NJG4 based at Juvincourt, north west of Reims, claiming a Halifax shot down at 2.57 over Reims at a height of 3800 metres. It was probably JB909, and his 12th victory. This pilot also claimed a Wellington bomber HE550 PT-G from 420 squadron, seven minutes earlier at 2.50am. This aircraft was also returning from Stuttgart, having taken off at 21.12 from Middleton St George, and shot down 5km south east of St. Quentin and crashing at Mesnil-St Laurent (Aisne). The pilot S/Ldr FV Taylor and F/O GC Crowther, both of the RCAF evaded capture. Two members of the crew, F/O S Brown, RCAF and P/O JA Simpson RCAF were sadly killed. Sgt HN McKinnon became a POW at Stalag Muhlberg-Elbe. The German pilot lost his life on 31 December 1944 aboard a Bf 109 G-10 near Hanover.

Significant Loss:

14.04.43 Fw. Rudolf Eisele	8./JG 2	⊤	☒ Our Flak: Brest	FW 190 A-5	WNr. 2634 -

Night: 14-15. April 143
R.A.F. Bomber Command: STUTTGART

15.04.43 Ltn. Heinz-Martin Hadeball	12./NJG 4	Wellington	☒ Mutterscheid: 5.400 m.	00.20	Film C. 2027/1 Anerk: Nr.2
15.04.43 Hptm. Floitgraf	11./NJG 4	Stirling	☒ Bibles bei Worms: 4,000 m.	00.21	Film C. 2027/1 Anerk: Nr.1
15.04.43 Hptm. Heinrich Wöhlers	Stab IV./NJG 4	Halifax II	☒ Niederlüstat: 5.000 m.	00.23	Film C. 2027/1 Anerk: Nr.93
15.04.43 Fw. Robert Lüddecke	5./NJG 2	Wellington	☒ 2637 / 07 Ost: no height	01.24	Film C. 2027/1 Anerk: Nr.94
15.04.43 Fw. Robert Lüddecke	5./NJG 2	Wellington	☒ 10 km. S.W. Korba: no height	01.43	Film C. 2027/1 Anerk: Nr.47
15.04.43 Ltn. Diaude	4./NJG 4	Wellington	☒ bei Yainville: 2.900 m.	01.46	Film C. 2027/1 Anerk: Nr.48
15.04.43 Hptm. Materne	4./NJG 4	Stirling	☒ 4 km. S.S.E. Sommerous: 2.000 m.	01.48	Film C. 2027/1 Anerk: Nr.20
15.04.43 Oblt. Rudolf Altendorf	2./NJG 4	Stirling	☒ 1 km. W. Fl.Pl. bei Charleville: 2.900 m.	01.50	Film C. 2027/1 Anerk: Nr.42
15.04.43 Oblt. Kurt Fladrich	9./NJG 4	Stirling	☒ 12 km. E. Reims: 3.300 m.	01.59	Film C. 2027/1 Anerk: Nr. -
15.04.43 Ofw. Reinhard Kollak	7./NJG 4	Lancaster	☒ 27 km. E. Reims: 3.000 m.	02.11	Film C. 2027/1 Anerk: Nr.35
15.04.43 Oblt. Rudolf Altendorf	2./NJG 4	Halifax	☒ 2 km. S.W. Eppe-Taurage: 5.100 m.	02.18	Film C. 2027/1 Anerk: Nr.21
15.04.43 Ltn. Fritz Gräff	Stab 1./NJG 4	Stirling	☒ 5 km. S.S.E. Namur: 3.400 m.	02.23	Film C. 2027/1 Anerk: Nr.35
15.04.43 Maj. Kurt Holler	Stab III./NJG 4	Stirling	☒ 20 km. N.E. St. Quentin: 3.700 m.	02.30	Film C. 2027/1 Anerk: Nr.26
15.04.43 Hptm. Hans-Karl Kamp	7./NJG 4	Wellington	☒ 5 km. E. St. Quentin: 3.800 m.	02.50	Film C. 2027/1 Anerk: Nr.36
15.04.43 Ltn. Helmut Bergmann	Stab III./NJG 4	Wellington	☒ 5 km. S.W. St. Quentin: 3.800 m.	02.55	Film C. 2027/1 Anerk: Nr.27
15.04.43 Hptm. Hans-Karl Kamp	7./NJG 4	Halifax	☒ 1 km. N. Reims: 3.800 m.	02.57	Film C. 2027/1 Anerk: Nr.37
15.04.43 Maj. Kurt Holler	Stab III./NJG 4	Wellington	☒ 2 km. N. Rocquiguer: 3.900 m.	02.58	Film C. 2027/1 Anerk: Nr.28
15.04.43 Hptm. Materne	4./NJG 4	Stirling	☒ 25 km. N.N.W. Châlons-sur-Marne: 400m	03.04	Film C. 2027/1 Anerk: Nr.LG
15.04.43 Ltn. Helmut Bergmann	Stab III./NJG 4	Halifax	☒ 15 km. S.W. St. Quentin: 3.100 m.	03.22	Film C. 2027/1 Anerk: Nr.29

15.04.43 Ltn. Horst Hannig	2./JG 2	Typhoon	☒ 2½km. N.N.W. Goderville: no height	17.00	Film C. 2027/1 Anerk: Nr. -
15.04.43 Hptm. Schumacher	2./NAG 13	Typhoon	☒ 4172 / 15 West: 2 -25 m.	20.28	Film C. 2027/1 Anerk: Nr.3

Jafü Holland-Ruhr

Supplemental Claims from Sources:

15.04.43 Ofw. Ernst Heesen: 31	5./JG 1	P-47	☒ -	17.40	Reference: JG 1 Lists f. 633
15.04.43 Ofw. Ernst Heesen: 32	5./JG 1	P-47	☒ -	17.40	Reference: JG 1 Lists f. 633

Significant Loss:

15.04.43 Oblt. Siegfried Graf von Matuschka	4./JG 54	KiA	☒ Spitfire: St. Inglevert	Bf 109 G-4	WNr. 19 222 -

16. April 143
U.S. VIII Bomber Command: LORIENT & BREST

16.04.43 Ofw. Friedrich May	8./JG 2	B-24D	☒ 20 km. N.W. Brest: 7.000 m.	13.36	Film C. 2027/1 Anerk: Nr.159
16.04.43 Ofw. Friedrich May	8./JG 2	B-24D	☒ 10 km. N.W. Brest: 2.000 m.	13.38	Film C. 2027/1 Anerk: Nr.160
16.04.43 Uffz. Ernst Henning	1./JG 2	Spitfire	☒ 25 km. N. Brest: 6.500 m.	13.45	Film C. 2027/1 Anerk: Nr. -
16.04.43 Hptm. Jürgen Hepe	1./JG 2	Spitfire	☒ 2 km. S.W. Plouguin: 7.000 [Finistère]	13.46	Film C. 2027/1 Anerk: Nr. -
16.04.43 Ofw. Josef Biggge	8./JG 2	B-24D	☒ 6925 / 14 West: 700 m.	13.56	Film C. 2027/1 Anerk: Nr.161
16.04.43 Ltn. Hans-Joachim Kinzel	Stab III./JG 2	B-17	☒ 4829 / 14 West: 8.000 m.	14.05	Film C. 2027/1 Anerk: Nr. -
16.04.43 Hptm. Egon Mayer	Stab III./JG 2	B-17	☒ 4829 / 14 West: 6.000 m.	14.05	Film C. 2027/1 Anerk: Nr. -
16.04.43 Hptm. Egon Mayer	Stab III./JG 2	B-17	☒ 4834 / 14 West: 1.000 m.	14.22	Film C. 2027/1 Anerk: Nr. -
16.04.43 Ltn. Josef Wurmheller	9./JG 2	B-17	☒ 4838 / 14 West: 6.000 m.	14.25	Film C. 2027/1 Anerk: Nr. -
16.04.43 Oblt. Ferdinand Müller	9./JG 2	B-17	☒ 5872 / 14 West: 6.500 m.	14.30	Film C. 2027/1 VNE: ASM
16.04.43 Ltn. Hans Schmidt	8./JG 2	B-17	☒ 7918 / 14 West: tiefflug	15.20	Film C. 2027/1 Anerk: Nr.162

Miscellaneous Interceptions:

16.04.43 Ltn. Horst Hannig	2./JG 2	Spitfire	☒ 45 km. N.N.W. St. Valéry: 6.000 m.	08.50	Film C. 2027/1 Anerk: Nr. -
16.04.43 Oblt. Günther Behrendt	11./JG 2	Typhoon	☒ 12 km. N. Pont Audemer: 2.500 m.	18.07	Film C. 2027/1 Anerk: Nr. -
16.04.43 Uffz. Heinz Buteweg	8./JG 2	Spitfire	☒ 5937 / 14 West: 50 m.	20.03	Film C. 2027/1 Anerk: Nr.163

Also shown is a schedule of German Night Fighters Claims matched to Bomber Command Losses for the 14th and 15th April, 1943.

There is absolutely no doubt that Ian MacKenzie thought of his crew first, and himself last. From eye witnesses there is also no doubt that he stayed with the burning bomber to avoid it crashing on houses in La Neuvillette. The villagers remembered. There is a fine memorial to this brave pilot. In a street named after him.

However, in spite of eye witness reports there was no award or decoration from the French Government; this remains a puzzle to the family of Ian MacKenzie.

German Night Fighter Claims Matched to Bomber Command Losses, 14-15

April 1943

Pilot	Unit	Claim	Location	Probable Victim
Lt Heinz Hadeball	12/NJG 4	Wellington, 0020 hrs	Mutterscheidt	HZ357/431 Sqn (Sgt L Denby)
Hptm Karl Floitgraf	11/NJG 4	Stirling, 0021 hrs	Biblis	BK709/7 Sqn (Plt Off J Mank)
Hptm Heinrich Wohlers (+ 15 Mar 44)	IV/NJG 4	Halifax, 0023 hrs	Niederlüstadt	HR678/35 Sqn (Plt Off R E Wilkes DFM)
Lt Franz Draude	4/NJG 4	Wellington, 0146 hrs	Joinville	X3763/425 Sqn (Plt Off A T Doucette DFC)
Hptm Otto Materne (+6 Aug 44)	4/NJG 4	Stirling, 0148 hrs	4 km SSE Sommesous	BF462/90 Sqn (Plt Off R J Beldin)
Oblt Rudolf Altendorf	2/NJG 4	Stirling, 0150 hrs	1 km W. of Charleville airfield	BF500/149 Sqn (Plt Off D B White)
Oblt Kurt Fladrich	9/NJG 4	Stirling, 0159 hrs	12 km E. of Reims	EF331/214 Sqn (Sgt L Powell)
Hptm Helmut Peters	III/NJG 101	Wellington, 0210 hrs		
Ofw Reinhard Kollak	7/NJG 4	Lancaster, 0211 hrs	27 km E.of Reims	
Oblt Rudolf Altendorf	2/NJG 4	Halifax, 0218 hrs	2 km SW Eppe-Sauvage	W4951/101 Sqn (Sgt R G Hamilton)
Lt Fritz Graeff	I/NJG 4	Stirling, 0223 hrs	5 km SSE Namur	BF513/75 Sqn (Plt Off D G McCaskill)
Maj Kurt Holler (+22 Jun 43)	III/NJG 4	Stirling, 0230 hrs	20 km NE St Quentin	Lancaster ED653/100 Sqn (Flt Lt R J Shufflebotham)
Hptm Hans-Karl Kamp (+31 Dec 44)	7/NJG 4	Wellington, 0250 hrs	5 km east of St Quentin	HE550/420Sqn (Sqn Ldr F V Taylor)
Lt Helmut Bergmann (+ 7 Aug 44)	7/NJG 4	Wellington, 0255 hrs	Dallon	HE733/425 Sqn (Sgt R B Dingman)
Hptm Hans-Karl Kamp	7/NJG 4	Halifax, 0257 hrs	1 km N Reims	JB909/408 Sqn (Plt Off I C Mackenzie)
Maj Kurt Holler (+22 Jun 43)	III/NJG 4	Wellington, 0258 hrs	2 km N Rocquigny	HE863/420 Sqn (Sgt P J Cozens)
Hptm Otto Materne (+6 Aug 44)	4/NJG 4	Stirling, 0304 hrs	25 km NNW Chalons-sur-Marne	Halifax DT746/10 sqn (Flt Sgt J E G Hancock)
Oblt Helmut Bergmann (+7 Aug 44)	7/NJG 4	Halifax, 0322 hrs	Tugny	BB311/408 Sqn (Plt Off L E Usher)

CHAPTER 5

REIMS

My father's account continues:

After being found and woken up by a German soldier, around 3.30am in a field east of Reims, (in the vicinity Cernay- les- Reims) I was handled roughly on to a farm cart to be taken to the nearest road. The jolting over the rough field was harrowing, particularly as my shattered right leg, with a compound fracture, just wobbled about at will over the side of the cart. My jaw was cracked, from shrapnel wound, and my face, right arm and leg were covered in blood. A van collected me and took me to Maison Blanche (the American Memorial Hospital built after WW1) now in German hands, in Reims. It was being used by the German military authorities as a convalescence home for badly wounded and frost bitten German soldiers from the Russian Front. I considered myself 'lucky' to have been shot down over French territory. If I had been shot down near the (bombed) target in Germany it is possible I might have been murdered by the Gestapo or hanged by a group of civilians. Wehrmacht and/or Luftwaffe personnel would try and capture downed aircrew before other elements of the Nazi regime.

I am unlikely to forget the 14/15th April, 1943. I lay on a stretcher in the hospital, bleeding profusely. My little world had been changed to one of utter despair and loneliness. After interrogation, where I gave my name, rank, number and next of kin I was transferred to a German army doctor and German army nurses. My wounds were dressed and a plaster cast fitted which virtually covered my entire right leg. In the midst of this chaos, an angel appeared - Madame Chatelin from the Reims Red Cross, she smiled and handed me some sweets and cigarettes. A little later a lovely French cleaning lady looked into my room, and when not being closely supervised, gathered me up in her arms and gave me a great big hug. This was very brave for two reasons; firstly, the guards were not slow at handing out punishment, at any sign of pro-British sentiment, and secondly I obviously looked revolting with dried blood over my right arm and face and blood still oozing from the undressed jaw wound. I shall always remember these two wonderful ladies.

On 23rd April, his diary records:

Leg very painful, not much sleep. Madame Chatelin came, with her 15 year old daughter Francoise, to see me. Germans told me I was not to see her anymore - MISERY!

After a few weeks an x-ray was taken which showed that the bone had failed to set. It also showed that there was a large piece of metal and over 100 smaller pieces in the leg. Over the years, after a hot bath the odd piece comes out, but they are not big enough to trigger the security alarm systems at airport on check in.

As so much of the cast had been removed, it was insufficiently rigid to hold the shattered pieces of bone together. A lengthy discussion took place, between the doctors, as to what action to take. I thought at this point that my leg might have to be amputated at just above the right knee. However, it was decided to have a further try, the wounds were dressed and a fresh cast fitted. The wounds were covered by the cast and just left to get on with it. My covered leg and the wounds became targets for bed bugs. These little creatures would crawl between the leg and the cast, and as they were undisturbed, just helped themselves. The itching became almost unbearable and resulted in many sleepless nights. These mites may possibly have saved my leg from becoming seriously infected or even gangrenous.

Several weeks later a further x-ray was taken which thankfully showed that the bones had set. The removed cast exposed the awful mess of the festering wounds. Shortly afterwards my leg became swollen, very hot and very painful. An operation was carried out to remove a large chunk of metal, which I found tied to my wrist when I woke up. His diary note of 2nd June sums up his despair, pain, fatigue, loneliness and hunger - 'When will it all end? Bed bugs are vicious and like me they are always hungry'.

My room in the hospital was large with a total of 4 beds. During my first week a Canadian flying officer joined me. He had a broken ankle on which a small cast was fitted, but he was totally mobile otherwise. He had managed to conceal a small hacksaw blade which the Germans failed to find; he started cutting through a window bar with a view to bending it sufficiently to enable him to crawl through. Although we were on the first floor, his aim was to knot his bedding and mine together and lower himself to the ground. He managed to get halfway through one bar, but was discovered by the Germans and immediately taken away. It is thought that visits by Madame Chatelin were stopped because of the attempted escape by the Canadian officer. The writer was informed by Eric Hebert that Madame Chatelin had, in fact, been arrested, with her husband on 20th July, 1943. They were interrogated by the Gestapo in Reims before being sent to the notorious prison in Fresnes, south of Paris, for further interrogation. They were eventually released, after two months.

While Mac was suffering physically from his ordeal, his parents in Dromara must have been devastated and distressed on receiving the official telegram in which he was reported missing on operations. A hand written telegram was also sent to Mrs.Worrell, his future mother in law, in Northwich, delivered 16th April. It read: Immediate from Air Ministry, Kingsway, P6570 16/4/43. Regret to inform you that Pilot Officer William Alexander McIlroy is reported missing as the result of air operations on the night of 14/15th April. Enquiries are being made through the International Red Cross Committee and any further information received will be communicated to you immediately. Stop. Should news of him reach you from any other source please advise this department. Stop. His father has been informed. Stop. Any other source could have referred to 'capture cards' which prisoners completed themselves, soon after capture and sent to relatives. Frequently, they are the first news that a man has become a POW. His father, Robert McIlroy, received the following letter from Wing Commander WDS Ferris, DFC, commanding officer of 408 Sqn, RCAF.

Dear Mr McIlroy,

Before you receive this letter you will have a signal informing you that your son 50572 Pilot Officer William Alexander McIlroy, has been reported missing as a result of air operations at approximately 9.15 pm on the night of the 14 instant, "Paddie" (as he was known to the boys and members of his crew) took off from this aerodrome to carry out operations over Stuttgart, Germany but unfortunately failed to return. He and his crew were due back at this aerodrome at approximately 5am the next morning but no news has been received from either the crew or the aircraft since the time of take-off.

It is with regret that I have to write to you this date to convey to you the feelings of my entire Squadron, the loss of your son in this Squadron is most deeply felt. He was an exceptionally good wireless operator air gunner and his cooperation with me was very commendable. He was keen and enthusiastic and set a wonderful example to other air crew members.

"Paddie" had a great number of very dear friends both on the Squadron and on the station. He had carried out his operational commitments under all circumstances and had deported himself in a very courageous manner. Your son had 27 operational trips to his credit and a total of 151 operational hours over enemy territory.

There is always a possibility that your son may be a prisoner of war, in which case, you will either hear direct or through Air Ministry who will receive advice from the International Red Cross Society. To be a prisoner of war is not the happiest thought in one's mind, particularly for you who was so fond of your son but on the other hand I hope you will bear with me that it carries gratifying thought in knowing that our loved ones are alive and well and will some day return home safely.

This war has caused grief to millions of people all over the world and it is a sorrowful state to know that so many fine young men must make great sacrifices in order to end and erase from the face of the earth an infuriated enemy whose jealousy and hatred of our spirit and strength will eventually crush him and the members of his country.

I do not wish to grieve you further in your deep anxiety, but trust that you will bear with us until such a time as definite information is received one way or the other concerning the welfare of your son.

Your sons affects have been gathered together and forwarded to the Commanding Officer, Central Depository, Colnbrook, Slough, Bucks and that Officer will communicate with you in the very near future.

Should there be any further information you require or anything in my power that I could do for you I would be only too pleased to comply with your wishes. If any further news of your son is received by my Squadron I can assure you I will convey same to you immediately.

May I offer my most sincere sympathies as well as those of my Officers and men in your anxiety.

About a week later, a letter from the Chaplain of 408 Sqn, HED Ashford, dated 24 April was delivered to the farm.

Dear Mr McIlroy,

It is with a heavy heart that I extend to you my sympathy over the word that you received in regard to your son "Paddy" (as he was known to his Squadron).

He was one of the most experienced Wireless Operators, and one of the best men we have ever had in the Squadron. Somehow or other, it never entered our minds that he would not finish his tour of operations. Perhaps it was our unwillingness to meet potential consequences that rendered us so sensitive to the shock.

We have not given him up, and we hope and pray that he shall yet be returned to our Squadron, and more especially to you, he so often spoke of his home and his loved ones. His pride in them was as great as his desire to do to the best of his ability, the task that was set to his hands. For many months I have seen him off on every operation and have had the great joy of welcoming him back. Now I still cherish the hope of welcoming him back sometime. Paddy was such a courageous man, the dangers to which he was exposed developed in him the highest type of courage that I have known.

Now my heart aches for you as his Chaplain. I cherish such a pride in him, that I can understand dimly, at least the sense of your great loss, courage such as he had must have been derived from those who gave him birth and from those who shared his life since birth. His personality and his influence do live on in the Squadron. We were so proud to have him and appreciate so much the splendid son you gave to the Air Force.

As a Chaplain I could ask for no higher reward than the simple privilege of knowing men such as he.

Now you are passing through the dark waters of stress and strain and anxiety. Your daily and hourly wait for the word that seems to come so slowly.

May God be very near to you at this time. May He be a light in your darkness and strength in your weakness and in His own way give you peace.

I cannot imagine the mental anguish of receiving such news and letters and it must have been absolutely awful and very depressing, for the Squadron CO and Chaplain to write such letters on a regular basis. In maybe 700 letters or more.

Around 8th May, 1943, my grandparents received a telegram, which was later confirmed by letter from the Air Ministry that he was in fact alive and a prisoner of war, in Reims Hospital.

Sir,

I am directed to confirm a telegram from this department in which you were notified that information has now been received through the International Red Cross Committee that your son P/O William Alexander McIlroy, Royal Air Force, is a prisoner of war, wounded.

The Committee's report quotes German information but does not give the address of the camp at which your son is located; he should, however, now be able to communicate this direct to you.

A pamphlet regarding communication with prisoners of war is enclosed as it may be of service to you. (Appendix 4)

Another letter later from the Red Cross.

Dear Mr McIlroy,

re: 50572 Pilot Officer W. McIlroy

We are officially informed by the Air Ministry that your son has been made a Prisoner of War and that he has been wounded. According to a cable from the International Red Cross Committee at Geneva he was in April in a hospital in Reims. This address is not we think sufficient for letters to be sent there and we advise that until you have further news you communicate with your son according to paragraph 2b of the leaflet PW/99b/42, which we herewith enclose.

No parcels should be despatched to your son at present, but in case you wish to prepare one, we are sending you the labels and clothing coupons so that you may have a parcel ready when you hear your son's camp address.

We hope you will soon have news of your son and shall be much obliged if you will let us know the address from which he writes.

We are well aware that this will be a time of considerable anxiety for you and are glad to be able to tell you that reports of hospital treatment for wounded Prisoners of War are excellent. This Organisation sends parcels of invalid comforts and diets to all hospitals where there are known to be British Prisoners of War and we trust that your son will be benefiting from these.

We hope our circulars will give you all the information you require and shall be glad to answer any queries.

My father's notes continue:

During the month of May, I received a letter from my Australian friend and room mate (at RAF

Leeming) Pilot Officer Derek Giblin, in which he confessed that he had taken my suit. This wasn't the only item that was 'borrowed' or stolen, when I was listed as missing; the kit I received back at the end of the war was deficient of many items. Interestingly enough, in October 1945 I met up with my wartime bat man in Carlisle, who admitted taking my shoes. I gave him full marks for courage in owning up to the theft, hoped they fitted well, and told him he was welcome to keep them. See appendix 5 for a bureaucratic conclusion about my father's kit, or lack of it!

While my father was gradually recovering from his many wounds, Sgt. Canter, the second (sprog) pilot was making his way back to England, with the help of the French resistance. On his return to England he made the following statement:

MOST SECRET

M.I.9/S/P.G. (-) 1294

EVADED CAPTURE IN FRANCE

The information contained in this report is to be treated as most secret

STATEMENT BY: R.127907 Sgt. CANTER, Wilfred Lloyd, 408 Sqn RCAF

Left: Gibraltar, 23rd June, 1943   Arrived: Liverpool, 29th June, 1943.

I was the second pilot of a Halifax aircraft which took off from RAF Leeming,(Yorks.) about 2200 hours on the 14th April,1943 to bomb STUTTGART. On the return flight we were attacked by a night fighter over REIMS and the aircraft caught fire. The order to bale out was given about 0330 hours, 15th April.

 The only member of the crew whose name I know was P/O MACKENZIE, RAAF (first pilot) who with the flight engineer was preparing to jump when I left the aircraft. The rear gunner, mid-upper gunner, and the wireless operator jumped before me. (Canter omitted to mention that another gunner, navigator and bomb aimer had also baled out before he did)

About five hours later, while hiding at a deserted farm house, I saw a German patrol with two prisoners. I could not identify them, but they may have been the bomb aimer and navigator. I came down about 0345 hours just N.W. of REIMS. My leg was broken just above the ankle and I was unable to walk. I gathered up my parachute and, covering it with the harness, I started crawling in search of a hiding place, there being no cover in the field where I had come down. I crawled for about a mile, resting frequently. There were numerous Germans searching the district on foot, in cars, and on motor cycles, as several aircraft had come down that night. There was also a German barracks in the vicinity.

Eventually I reached two small deserted farm houses, in one of which I hid after climbing in through a window. During the day I called to two women who approached the house. I speak a little French, and I explained to them that I was RAF and asked for help. In the late afternoon the women brought me food and clothing- I was wearing shoes under my flying boots   – and took away my uniform. In the evening their husbands escorted me by bicycle to the home of one of them in REIMS, where I was sheltered for nine days (15-24 April) I was then handed over to an organisation which arranged the rest of my journey.

[Escape Report No 1294 (PRO (WO 208/3314)] 30th June,1943

The full report, shown in appendix 6 shows distribution of this report to various agencies and interested parties.

There is a little information available about the remainder of Canter's journey. The Comete Line was a line from Brussels through to Paris and onto Saint-Jean de Luz, a small fishing port in the shadow of the Pyrenees, near the Spanish border. Comete did not operate in Reims so aircrew shot down in the Reims area were sent to Paris. Madam Chatelin occasionally did the journey from Reims to Paris, but I have been informed that she was more of a co-ordinator for the French resistance. She did not know whether she met Canter or not and most of the couriers between Reims and Paris were arrested many being deported to Germany. The fate of many remains unknown.

Canter was taken to Paris by Madeleine Bouteloupt. She used to go from Montparnasse station in Paris to catch a train to Bordeaux, a journey of about 14 hours. In Bordeaux she handed Canter to Franco 'le passeur'.(mountain guide) Madeleine would return to Paris, and Franco with his 'charges' would catch a train to Dax (between Bordeaux and Saint-Jean de Luz) From Dax, Franco and the evaders would cycle the 50 Km to Saint-Jean, and stay at a safe house, probably organised by a Madam de Greef. The route to the border, from Saint-Jean followed a rough track/ road to a farmhouse at Urrugne, a distance of about 2.5 miles. If the weather was poor, as it often was, the evaders would stay overnight, leaving the next evening with Florentino Gioccaechea, a

Basque guide and smuggler. The success of completing their journey depended on crossing the river Bidossa and avoiding Spanish and Vichy French/German patrols. When on Spanish territory, where they were still in danger of being arrested, arrangements were made for the evaders to be collected and taken to the British Consulate in San Sebastian. Canter was very lucky because on the 15th May,1943 a traitor Jean Masson (real name – Desoubrie, from Tourcoing, in Belgium) joined the Comete Line and many helpers and aircrew were arrested. Madeleine Bouteloupt, was exposed by this traitor in Paris. On the 7th June, she was arrested on a train by the German Secret Police. She was deported and sadly died a few weeks after her liberation, from Ravensbruck. "Franco" is still alive and lives in Italy. He is Baron Jean Francoise Nothomb, son of a Belgian senator and writer. He took over the organising of the Comete Line after its founder, Dedee (Andree de Jongh) was arrested by the Gestapo. She survived the horrors of concentration camps and continued her work as a nurse after the war ended.

Thanks to the exceptional bravery and courage of members/helpers of the Comete Line, many aircrew were able to evade capture. This courage must never be forgotten. In Canter's case there was an added danger. He was Jewish and one can only speculate what his fate may have been if captured. Canter, on his return to England was awarded the DFM and volunteered to resume operations. It was most unusual for any aircrew who had been shot down and evaded capture to be allowed to continue operational flying. The reason was simply that the airman may be shot down again and, under interrogation, compromise the work of the French Resistance and Comete Line. He joined 433 Sqn. RCAF, and was shot down a second time on 23rd April, 1944 on a mission to Dusseldorf. He was flying a Halifax 111 HX 291, which was attacked by an (unseen) fighter. He became a POW and survived. After the war he served in the Israeli Air Force in the Israeli War of Independence, but was killed on 24th October, 1948. Flying Dakotas in 101 Sqn, an engine caught fire after take off for a night supply operation, and the aircraft exploded in flight.

From Royal Australian Air Force records the WOP/AG, Con O'Connell managed to stay free for 8 days. He reached Paris but was captured in the early hours of 21st April, as he was leaving the city. Taken prisoner, he was placed in Fresnes prison on suspicion of being a saboteur, and kept in solitary confinement for six weeks. The report shows that he received one bowl of soup a day, 3 slices of bread, and a bowl of coffee in the mornings. He states that he was given the "third" degree to tell who had given him a civilian coat. He was finally released and sent to Stalag Luft 111. In spite of a flesh wound on his right leg he was given no medical treatment.

F/S Stuart Murray, seriously injured in his right hand was, unbeknown to my father, also taken to the Memorial hospital. My father does not recall seeing him there. Murray was not a "regular" member of the crew. He was a replacement for P/O Rod Ball RCAF, who it is believed was on leave. Ball was shot down on 20th June on a mission to "Le Creusot", and became a POW at Stalag Luft 111. The other members of the crew, who were not wounded, Tiny Playfair, Tommy Coupland, and Lloyd McKenzie were sent to Courcy, then onto POW camps. McKenzie went to Stalag Kopernikus, the other two to Stalag Luft 111.

My father's notes continue:

At the end of July, 1943 I became aware that another pilot officer was in the room across the corridor from me. We tried to shout across to each other, but without much success. His name was Alex Ager, a Lancaster pilot with 101 Squadron, based at Ludford Magna. He had been shot down on the return leg of an operation to Cologne. His plane was attacked by a night fighter and crashed at Marly-Gomant (Aisne) 14km from ENE of Guise, France. Five of the crew sadly lost their lives of which one, Sgt G W Lloyd was, at the age of 17, one of the youngest airmen killed in Bomber Command Service. Alex suffered a broken thigh. His diary records the following:

13th August - Slept well, but was bitten by mosquitoes. Have been here 5 weeks. Home seems to be very dear to me now.

14th August - Mac was yelling this morning when the masseur got to work. I am to suffer next.

16th August - German guards very angered this morning, probably the boys have bombed their home town. Two Russian POWs are together in the next room, singing and laughing. Why are Mac and I separated?

20th August - Saw Mac walking this morning. Probably hear him swear.

6 September - Many aircraft heard in the night overhead. British aircraft on the way to Germany, accompanied by sirens and gunfire. Perhaps the Second Front has started.

Alex was visited several times by Madame Chatelin. He recalled that she brought him small cakes and grapes. Alex saved the grape pips and lined them up on the first floor window sill. He would then ping them down on the German guards below. He told me that this was the only way he could "shoot" the Germans. His actions irritated them and resulted in having no more grapes.

My father had two birthdays in captivity. The first, 17 September, 1943 was here in Reims. He recorded what he had to eat.

Breakfast: 1 cup of mint tea, 2 slices German bread with jam, no butter.

Lunch: 3 potatoes, small portion of cabbage.

Tea: 2 slices of bread, with blood sausage and margarine.

Dinner: Nothing.

Late supper: None and no cigarettes.

Alex's diary continues;

26th September - Reims bombed in daylight by a force of American bombers. It is good to hear the 'Old Forts' again.

9th October - Mac has 2 Russian POWs and a French convict in his room. Lucky dog to have company.

15th October - Today, Mac was transferred to my room. Cheers. We talked all day without a stop.

16th October – Marvellous for someone to talk to. Don't care now if I am here for Christmas. Lots of joy. We play battleships, noughts and crosses, etc.

My father's notes continue:

Alex was brought up in London and his background could not have been more different to mine. As a sophisticated city lad, he appeared to know, or have been to every decent restaurant in London. Our obsession with food, and civilisation generally, prompted Alex to list all the hotels and restaurants that we should visit when the war was over. These were all written in my POW scrap books and listed in Appendices 7 and 8 and for good measure, Alex recommended wines for different courses. His recommendations appear in Appendix 9

Alex and my father did stay in Reims for Christmas. They were in fairly high spirits, all things considered, but not in the best of physical health. But both of them were now mobile. Christmas and New Year came and went. He didn't record what they had to eat on Christmas Day, and their 'mobility' meant one thing - Alex and he weren't going to be staying in Reims much longer. On 4 January, 1944, they left Reims for incarceration in Eastern Germany - Silesia. His diary records: Goodbye Reims Alex and I are off to the 'cooler'. My memory of hospital will be pain, hunger and bed bugs.

The next time he visited Reims was in 1965, on his way to a holiday in Switzerland. The next visit after this was May, 2005 of which more later.

CHAPTER 6

STALAG LUFT III (BELARIA) JAN 1944 - JAN 1945

Mac's train journey, under armed guard from Reims, with Alex Ager, was, to say the least, unpleasant. He knew they were destined for a POW camp, Stalag Luft III, but met with considerable hostility from German military personnel and civilians, while travelling. Not surprising, really. RAF Bomber Command 'Terrorfliegers' were the only allied force continuously on active operations against Germany, from Day One. The armed guard kept them "safe" on their journey eastwards to Oberursel, near Frankfurt-am-Main. Here there was a reception camp, for RAF aircrew prisoners, called a Dulag Luft from the German word Durchgangslager (It means a Transit Camp or Entrance Camp). Slow progress was made to this camp, as their three day journey was continuously diverted to other tracks because of previous attacks.

The camp had three compounds, an interrogation centre at Oberursel, a transit camp at Wetzlar and a hospital at Hohemark. The interrogation centre comprised of four wooden buildings, two of which were each divided into roughly one hundred sound proofed isolation cells. A quarter of the cells contained eavesdropping devices. All cells were equipped with electric heaters, instead of radiators and hot water pipes, to prevent POWs contacting each other by Morse Code.

Mac and Alex checked in with quite a number of aircrew lads. Alex was POW number 3234. Mac was number 3267. They were admitted in alphabetical order, in typical German fashion and efficiency. They were both thoroughly searched even though they had been in "custody" for many months. Records were created and photographs taken. They were then taken to the "cooler" (solitary confinement) and dumped in there for "hot and cold" loosening up treatment. Some of the cells had been converted into "hotboxes" with asbestos lined walls where POWs were made to suffer very high temperatures in order to induce them to be co-operative. As noted in Mac's scrap book "not the nicest place on earth". Interrogation sessions were conducted by the Luftwaffe. Aboard German bombers, the navigator was the 'skipper'. The pilot was the 'driver'. Hence interrogators concentrated on navigators and wireless operators because not only did they tell the pilot where to fly but they had the most detailed knowledge of operational procedures and equipment. However, in the case of my father, his knowledge was nine months out of date. And he did not tell them anything anyway.

After several days, during which Alex and he tried to humour each other, they were despatched (East) by cattle truck, with others, to Belaria, between Berlin and Breslau in Prussian Silesia, very close to the Polish border. Belaria was an overflow compound at Sagan, which is now in present day Poland. (Zagan)

Stalag Luft 111 was built a year before my father was shot down and was the main camp for British and Allied aircrew. Originally built with two compounds, a Centre one for RAF NCOs and an East compound for officers, there were six by the end of the war. The camp was built on soft sand at the edge of a dense pine forest and enclosed by two lines of barbed wire about 12 feet high. About 15 feet inside the main wire was a single strand of barbed wire, placed about 12 inches off the ground. This was a warning wire and any POW stepping over it was liable to be shot. Even to touch it while, for example, walking round the compound boundary was likely to bring a warning shot from a nearby 'goon box.' Arc lights hung above the main wire and guard boxes – small towers on stilts- stood at all the corners and at regular intervals around the perimeter. Each tower was manned by two guards and each had a powerful searchlight to pan over the camp. The guards were armed with machine guns and had a telephone connection to the guardroom by the main gates. Armed soldiers patrolled the perimeter wire between each tower.

Inside the 'wire' were the single storey, green painted wooden barrack huts placed on piles about two feet above the ground. Each hut measured approximately 160 feet by 40 feet and divided into rooms where initially there were 8 bunks per room. All the windows had blackout shutters and each hut had a small kitchen and a very basic toilet, known as the 'Thunderbox' The so-called 'Stalag Lufts' were 'managed' by the Luftwaffe. .

Stalag Luft III housed 12,000 British and American aircrew officers. Alex and he thought it was crowded, but the Russians later stuffed 143,000 German POWs into it.

On their arrival at the gate, and this was common for all new arrivals, there was a reception committee. Father's scrap book records the following:

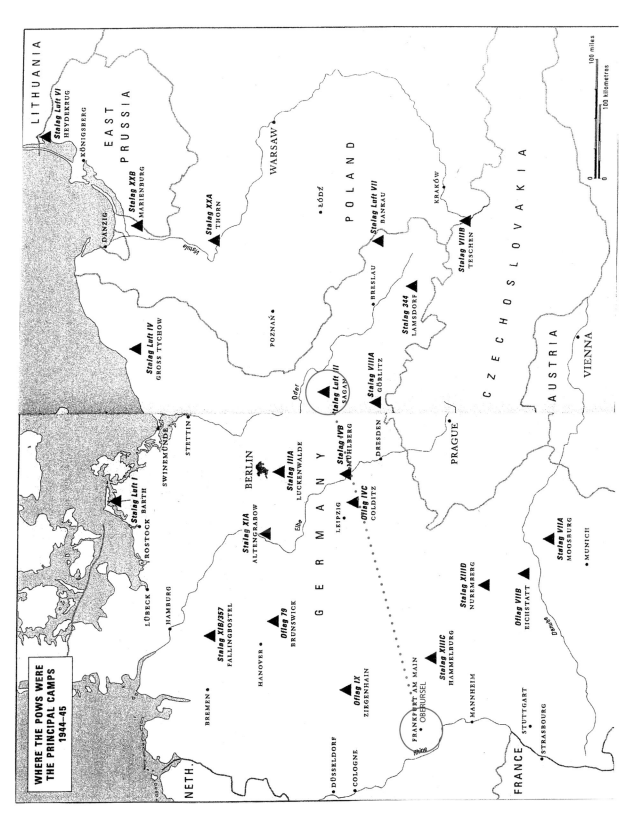

3. Principal POW Camps, 1944/45

The arrival at our prison camp, on 18th January, is a most unusual experience, while waiting at the gate for permission to enter, a large number of half naked people can be seen running out of doors and jumping through windows, from inside the barbed wire, giving us an impression of lunacy. However, we were not left for long in doubt as to the meaning of this performance as cries of "Hello, there is Old George, I wonder where he got shot down" or again "See fellows, I don't know anyone in this purge - isn't it pathetic. I guess we were Kriegies when these new chaps were civilians" were heard from this amazing assembly. (The German for POW was Kriegsgefangenen) These remarks filtering through the wire to us newly shot down, weary, travel stained, hungry, unshaven resemblances of better days, in the familiar accents of Canada, America, Britain and Australia, had the effect of raising our spirits tremendously and upon seeing such an array of people waiting to welcome us, it was hard not to feel a little flattered and to give oneself a mental pat on the back and think "I got shot down too".

This mental satisfaction did not last for long though as very soon we found that the old prisoners were simply there to obtain the latest news from home and when such questions as "When is the invasion to start" or "How long do you think the war will last", were not answered to their full satisfaction. It was no good getting offended when you were referred to as a particularly clueless bunch.

One learns eventually that the 'Old Kriegie' is a really generous individual with peculiar moods and interests and the apt but well worn Kriegiedom phrase of "Round the bend" sums him up in a nutshell.

Nine months in Reims Hospital made my father as news starved as they were. Alex and father were allocated to different huts. Alex went to 'Inglenook', named after the senior officer in charge, Wg. Cdr Ingle.

My father was allotted to eighth place upper bunk in BLOCK 4 ROOM 15 of the so called Mehargs

Mansion, and as more prisoners arrived, two further 2 tier bunks were added.

The seven officers already in residence were a very mixed bunch. There were two Spitfire pilots,

one Mustang pilot and four aircrew from Bomber Command. They all had different and very

difficult journeys to relate of how they arrived at Sagan.

F/O Joe Pakeman (Joe No.1) was a Halifax navigator with 76 Squadron, based at RAF Holme-on-

Spalding Moor. He was shot down by a night fighter (Hptm Eckart-Wilhelm von Bonin of 11./

NJG1) on 21st December, 1943 and the plane crashed 14 km. south east of Koblenz on the return

leg of a mission to Frankfurt.

F/Lt Geoff Evans was a fellow crew member of Joe Pakeman. Evans was the Signals Leader and

had taken the place of the crew's regular wireless operator, Sgt. B Williams. Geoff had a scar on

one of his lungs and smoked heavily while a POW, to make himself ill. He was subsequently repatriated. My father saw him after the War and he was very well. He was one of two 'Evans' in 4-15 and as he occupied a bottom bunk he was known as 'good evans'

F/Lt Johnny Brace was a Bomb Aimer, also with 76 Squadron. He was shot down over France on 13th August, 1943 on an operation to Milan. One of two survivors, he parachuted down to Bernay (EURE – Northern France). In his report he "attempted evasion on arrival. Contacted the French Resistance people on 13th August and eventually proceeded, by Paris and Ruffec to the Spanish frontier. Captured on a train between Toulouse and Biarritz with three Americans – Lt Toft, Sgt Klump, and Sgt Vandegriff, by German police on 20th November, 1943. I spent four weeks in Fresnes prison, Paris. Interrogated by the Gestapo and threatened with being treated as a spy as I was wearing civilian clothes. Sent to Dulag Luft, Frankfurt, arriving 16th December with the three Americans. Interrogated by a Luftwaffe officer"

P/O Reg Evans was a Lancaster pilot with 44 Squadron (Rhodesia) based at RAF Dunholme Lodge. The aircraft crashed at Rossdorf, Germany on an operation to Frankfurt, on 21st December, 1943. Reg and the wireless operator, Sgt Bateman, were the only survivors. Reg occupied a top bunk and was known as 'evans above'.

F/O Lesley Prickett was a Spitfire pilot with 41 Squadron, based at RAF Friston, Sussex. As a Sergeant he crash landed his plane at RAF Manston, Kent on 25th July, 1942. He was low on fuel after a 'Rhubarb' (small scale freelance fighter sortie against ground targets of opportunity) mission over France. Over a year later, on 27th August he was shot down by an FW 190 of German Base JG26 in the St.Pol area (west of Arras) France. With the help of the French Resistance he managed to evade until 17th December, 1943 where he was captured in Paris. Interrogated by the Gestapo in Fresnes prison he was eventually sent to Sagan, arriving on 10th January, 1944.

P/O Anthony Griffiths was a Spitfire pilot with 501 Squadron, based at RAF Martlesham Heath, east of Ipswich, Suffolk. He was on a 'Ramrod' mission (escorting Bomber aircraft to bring enemy fighters into combat but also with the intention of destroying a target) but unfortunately was shot down by a P-47 Thunderbolt of the USAAF on 21st December, 1943 near Abbeville, France. He was wounded and immediately captured. After interrogation he arrived in Sagan on 10th January, 1944.

F/Lt Maurice Wilson was a regular Army Officer with the Army Co-operation Command, before transferring to the RAF and becoming a Mustang pilot. He was shot down on 18th January, 1943 near Abbeville but evaded capture. Assisted by the French Resistance, he was "passed" down the O'Leary line but was captured by plain clothes police 15 miles south of Perpignan on 13th June. He had evaded for five months. Interrogated by the Gestapo in Boulou, near the Spanish border, he was transferred to Fresnes prison, Paris. A post war letter, dated 1st August, 1946 (written in French) and sent from Paris to M I 9 and signed by Fabien de Cortes with PA O/Leary shows the amazing display of courage of Maurice Wilson before he was eventually sent to Sagan on 10th January, 1944.

The letter (translated) is as follows;

During the night of 12/13th June 1943, I was arrested in the region of Boulou together with F/O MHG Wilson (then an RAF pilot) and Mr. Pierre Ryckebusch.

As I had escaped from the Gestapo only six weeks previously, I obviously could not give my real name. I therefore passed myself off as a RCAF airman who had been shot down in occupied territory, as did Mr.Ryckebusch. For this purpose, F/O Wilson was of invaluable help to us, in giving us all the information we needed in order to persuade our German interrogators that this story was true.

Thanks to this help, we were able to maintain this story for more than three months, and when the Gestapo finally discovered the truth it was too late for them to arrest the other members of the organisation who helped us on our journey.

I would like to state that at all times, F/O Wilson's demeanour was courageous and patriotic during the interrogations he underwent. In his replies to the Gestapo (22, Avenue Foch, Paris) he kept strictly to the plan we had evolved of saying absolutely nothing to the Germans that might put them on the trail of the organisation.

I also know that even when he was beaten, he still refused to give a single detail that might have helped the Gestapo to find the people who had helped him during his stay in France.

During our imprisonment in Fresnes, F/O Wilson was a most loyal and devoted friend and companion in the cell we shared.

Signed: Fabien de Cortes/ PA O'Leary.

A postscript was written by O'Leary as follows:

I would like to draw the attention of the authorities to the exceptionally brave attitude of F/O Wilson, who in order to save the escape organisation which had taken care of him, agreed to eventually renounce his rights as a POW by upholding the two agents with him.

These seven gentlemen welcomed my father into the hut with a cup of German tea and some homemade cake, which consisted of dubious constituents, but was appreciated, nevertheless, after starvation rations at the hospital and the long train journey. My father eventually met up with three crew members who had been incarcerated in Belaria. Tiny Playfair (Navigator) and Tommy Coupland (Bomb Aimer) since April, 1943 and Con O'Connell, the Australian wireless operator since June, 1943. They were surprised but pleased to see him and that he had survived his serious injuries. Lloyd McKenzie, the Canadian flight engineer had been sent to Stalag Kopernikus. F/ Sgt Murray, the Canadian mid upper gunner who lost half his right hand was to be repatriated in September, 1944. It is not known which camp (if any) he was sent to after hospital treatment. Sagan was well known for its escaping activities. It was a camp for airforce officers and airmen aircrew of all allied nationalities, and the 'tally ho' boys were always active in making attempts to escape. Since the camp opened, the Germans had recorded 262 escape attempts, 100 involving tunnels. Every snippet of information obtained was passed on. POWs and the German guards who patrolled inside the wire – known as ferrets- often had conversations from which much useful escape information was elicited. Bill Lott told me of the following: A ferret who normally appeared every day in the compound did not appear for a week. On his return a POW would greet him with "what-ho, thought you had been sent to fight the Russians". It then transpired that the guard had been on leave and was easily persuaded to whinge about the difficulties of public transport on his journey from Sagan, to say, Leipzig, resulting in his only being able to spend two days with his family. Note for escapers: don't head for Leipzig. Most escape attempts required materials, particularly wood. One source of this valuable commodity were bed boards, of which the main use was to line escape tunnels. Alex Ager told me that, without his knowledge, only three boards on his bed were left to support the straw mattress and himself. One night, while lying on his top bunk, it collapsed and he landed on the POW below. The POW was knocked out by one of the remaining boards. A number of bunks had no boards at all and the occupant was obliged to tie the corners of their mattress to the bed posts and make do with the resulting 'hammock'.

The Wooden Horse escape in 1943 was immortalised in a film of that name, where 3 escapees made it home. My father was generally unfit throughout his time at Stalag Luft III and was excused tunnel digging. At one stage his leg became excessively swollen and inflamed. A British Army doctor - also a prisoner, heated the blade of a penknife, and made a slit in his leg to allow the pus to ooze out, so relieving the pressure. His leg was then packed with gauze to allow it to drain completely.

POWs continuous attempts to escape from Stalag Luft 111 (and other camps) prompted the authorities to issue directives concerning POW escapees. In February, 1944, Himmler, head of the Central Security Headquarters implemented Stufe Romisch 111. This directive required all recaptured POWs to be handed over to the Gestapo and not returned to Luftwaffe custody. No other authority or organisation, such as the Red Cross or POW committees were to be advised of such action.

In March, a further directive was implemented, called Aktion Kugel (Operation Bullet) This decreed that all recaptured POWs, except British and American, were to be sent to Mauthausen Concentration Camp, and executed.

In addition to these 'murderous' directives, attempts to escape prompted the authorities to install equipment such as seismographs to detect earth movements and tunnelling activities. According to BA 'Jimmy' James (Moonless Night) the Germans "even engaged a water diviner, imagining he might be able to locate tunnels. An old man with a drooping moustache, he wandered along outside the wire, his hazel rod waving vaguely in front of him. Shadowed by a derisive crowd of prisoners, he stopped opposite every block except 104" Block 104 contained the entrance to "Harry", the most famous tunnel of the War.

In April 1944, the German authorities announced that the officers (whose photographs are shown) who escaped from North Camp - Stalag Luft III were now dead.

This was the Great Escape where 76 escaped on the 24th March 1944

After the mass escape a Grossfahndung (National Alert) was issued on the highest authority. All security forces were placed on full alert throughout Germany, and an SS Panzer division, located in the Sagan area.

When Hitler was informed he was incensed and ordered, after a meeting with Himmler, Goring and Keitel that all officers recaptured were to be executed. Because reprisals might be taken against German prisoners captured by the allies, Himmler, with Hitler's approval, limited the number to be shot to fifty. Roger Bushell, a South African born Barrister who had been commanding 92 Squadron (Spitfires) in France, was Big X on the Escape Committee, and Schneidauer, a French pilot officer, were shot near an autobahn on their way to Kaiserslautern. They had been interrogated at the Gestapo Headquarters in Saarbrucken. Over the next two weeks, another 71 were recaptured. Out of 76 escapees, only three managed to get back to England. Eight were sent to Concentration Camps and only 15 were returned to Stalag Luft III.

The price was very high for this escape.

A post war tribunal investigating the 'Sagan Murders' raised the possibility that the Nazi authorities were aware of the existence of the tunnel 'Harry'. Aside from the water diviner seismographic equipment had been taken away for 'maintenance work' The Nazis allowed the escape to take place and by implementing 'Operation Bullet', a barbaric example was made to deter all further attempts to escape.

One of the officers shot was F/Lt EG Brettell, RAF, who wrote the following whilst incarcerated in the 'Cooler' at Gross Hartmannsdorf, Saxony in April, 1943.

ESCAPE

If you can quit the compound undetected

And clean your tracks not leave the smallest trace,

And follow out the programme you've selected

Not lose your grasp of distance, time and space…..

If you can walk at night by compass bearing

Or ride the railways in the light of day

And temper your elusiveness with daring

Trusting that sometimes bluff will find a way

If you can swallow sudden sour frustrations

And gaze unmoved at failures ugly shape

Remembering, as further inspiration

It was and is your duty to escape

If you can keep the great Gestapo guessing

With explanations only partly true

And leave them in the heart of hearts confessing

They did not get the whole truth out of you

If you can use your "Cooler" fortnight clearly

For planning methods wiser than before

And trust your first miscalculations merely

As hints let fall by fate, to teach you more

If you can scheme on with patience and precision

It wasn't in a day they builded Rome

And make escapes your single sole ambition

The next time you attempt it – you'll get home

Posters were put up in all areas of the camp. All POWs must not consider escape as a sport. All German guards have been given direct orders to shoot all suspected persons trying to escape. Escape must not be attempted.

Camp morale dropped on the news of this mass murder. My father's scrap book records the following:

There was a memorial service on 13 April, 1944 in Camp Belaria, "in honour of our brave comrades who died while performing their duty"

Officer Commanding

Attention - Remove Head dress - Stand at ease

Hymn. Oh God our help in ages past

Prayer

Psalm 23

Prayer

Response

Rest eternal grant unto them. O Lord and let light perpetual shine upon them.

Prayers

The Lesson

The Address

Hymn God of our Fathers, known of old

Officer Commanding

Attention - Replace head dress

Last Post - Officers commanding blocks and supernumeries at the salute during the sounding of the Last Post.

Reveille

They shall grow not old

As we that are left grow old

Age shall not weary them

Nor the years condemn

At the going down of the sun

And in the morning

We will remember them

[Lawrence Robert Binyon's elegy 'For The Fallen' 1914-1918]

The service was very moving.

Great solidarity amongst us all. Every man must have wondered, as I did, if we were going to survive all this. Would we ever get home? How will it end? Camp life was monotonous. Being a POW is aptly described by Winston Churchill, when he was a Prisoner of War in South Africa in 1899 -

It is a melancholy state, you are in the power of the enemy, you owe your life to his humanity, your daily bread to his compassion. You must obey his orders, await his pleasure, possess your soul in patience. Meanwhile the war is going on, great events are in progress, fine opportunities for action and adventure are slipping away. Also

the days are very long. Hours crawl by like paralytic centipedes. Nothing amuses you. Reading is difficult; writing impossible. Life is one long boredom from dawn to slumber. Moreover the whole atmosphere of prison, even the most easy and best regulated of prisons, is odious. Companions in this kind of misfortune quarrel about trifles at and get the least possible pleasure from each others society. If you have never been under restraint before and never known what it was to be a captive, you feel a sense of constant humiliation in being confined to a narrow space, fenced in by railings and wire, watched by armed men, and webbed about with a tangle of regulations and restrictions.

My father's notes did not record this passage in full

There was little to do, except talk of food and freedom. Freedom was uppermost in their minds. For a start, it meant food. The vicious reprisals of the "Great Escape" curbed enthusiasm, but only for a while. The thought of a really decent meal prompted him to write in his 'scrap book' a considerable number of menus and recipes contributed by many of his fellow inmates.

(Appendix 10) There was, of course, little chance to produce most of them. There's a limit to what you can do with the rations available.

German issues of food for one week was:

5oz Sugar	2oz Ersatz Cheese
2oz Synthetic Jam	2oz Fresh Meat
1 Loaf - Dark Brown	1oz Sausage (Blutworst)
30 Potatoes	Ersatz Tea
Turnips or Swedes	Salt
Cooked Barley	Occasional dry vegetables

German issued utensils:

1 Fork	1 Bowl
1 Knife	1 Kanne Trinkwasser
1 Spoon	1 Porcelain Jug
1 Cup	1 Basin

Pots and pans for cooking were not issued by the Germans, so these very necessary items are supplied through the kindness of the Canadians POW Relatives Association. Other utensils, such as plates, coffee percolators are made by ourselves from various types of tins - principally cocoa tins. The chief utensil creator in his hut was Flying Officer L.A. Prickett. (a former pupil of Worksop College, Notts)

Red Cross parcels (cardboard boxes) were a very important part of life. Contents listed in Appendix (11) Due to the combined efforts of the British, Canadian, American and New Zealand Red Cross, each prisoner was issued with one Red Cross parcel per week which, added to the meagre German allowance, "makes ones life in a prisoner of war camp fairly comfortable, as far as the food question is concerned". Provided we received them. However, it was very rare to receive one parcel per week. Even in good times, two parcels a month was exceptional. As the war continued, the number of POWs increased. This situation combined with misappropriation and damage (by Bomber Command) to depots and distribution routes meant that the Red Cross parcels did not always get to the camps. The erratic supply meant that the pangs of hunger were there all the time.

Unbeknown to him, his sister in Ireland, Edith had tried to send him parcels to Reims. News travelled slowly and she was obliged to include the contents of any parcel with the quarterly parcel that her father sent. A letter dated 28 January 1944 from the Next of Kin Parcels Centre, 14 Finsbury Circus, London, EC2 explains.

Dear Madam,

Re: Pilot Officer W A McIlroy 50572

We have received the parcel which you sent to your brother and have been able to connect it up with the previous one as this was being held over because there was some difficulty about forwarding it to the American Hospital, Rheims.

Will you kindly note, however, that we are not able to accept parcels except under our special label which is issued once every three months and according to our Records No.13 label and coupons are held by Mr McIlroy. If you wish to send anything to your brother in future will you please include them in your father's quarterly parcel.

We have had to return the tube of toothpaste which you sent as collapsible tubes are prohibited in the next-of-kin parcel as you will see from the instructions sent with the label. We also have to return the letter intended for Pilot Officer McIlroy as the only way this can be sent is by letter post in the usual way.

When she had received this letter, my father had already left Reims.

His sister received a further letter, from the War Organisation of the Red Cross Society, dated 9 June, 1944. It would seem that it was possibly the first time that the family knew he was in Stalag Luft III. She must have caused a stir by mentioning another POW Camp, as the letter highlights:

Dear Miss McIlroy,

re: <u>50572 Pilot Officer W. McIlroy</u>

You will remember that when your brother was first known to be a Prisoner of War, a message was sent to him by cable from this Office to be delivered through the International Red Cross Committee at Geneva. We have now received a notification from the International Red Cross Committee that your brother is interned at Stalag 3 and that the message has been forwarded to him. Further news of his condition is being requested. We hope you have yourself received letters from your brother and that he is better.

We understand from our Packing Centre that the parcel which you recently despatched to him bore two addresses, Stalag Luft 3 and Bibarach Riss. We would be much obliged if you would let us know from what source you obtained the second address. In any case, your brother is definitely not at that camp and you should continue to send all letters and parcels to him addressed to Stalag Luft 3, Prisoner of War number 3267.

Next of Kin parcels could be sent quarterly via the POW organisation which checked the contents and repacked them.. Chocolate was the only food item allowed in these parcels. It was felt unfair if the recipient of one of these parcels had access to more food than other POWs.

From 11 September 1944, rations were cut to half a Red Cross parcel per week and soon afterwards supplies became very erratic. The thought of a slap-up meal was never far from their thoughts. They had the recipes!

After a 'meal', there was nothing like a good smoke, if available, although he had to wait until 11 October 1944 for his first tobacco parcel. 4oz arrived from the Ardath Tobacco Co Ltd, Worship Street, London, EC2. A Mr L Speirs of 147 Marsham Court, Marsham Street, London, SW1 had kindly paid for it. Tobacco parcels, provided they had been paid for, were sent direct from the manufacturer to the POW.

His address was quite straightforward

P/O W A McIlroy 50572

Prisoner of War, 3267

Stalag Luft III

Germany

Apart from thoroughly appreciating it, tobacco (with food) was a trading currency. Some smoked more, and ate less, than others. There was, in fact, a camp currency – Kriegsgefangenen Lagergeld. Under the terms of the Geneva Convention relative to the Treatment of Prisoners of War, Allied authorities were permitted to forward up to 20% of an officers pay, via the Red Cross, to the POW. The hard currency received was converted by the Germans to Lagergeld. It could only be spent inside the camp. In Mac's scrap book are three entries referring to 'Money Transferred to my bank account from Reichmarks', as follows

June 1944   £16-08-0

October 1944   9-00-00

January 1945   71-00-00

To help while away the hours, he read a lot of the books that were available, many supplied by the YMCA (Appendix 12) .He would never have read all those books in normal circumstances. The YMCA had book distribution centres in Switzerland and Sweden and these centres were also used by the Red Cross. Similar to the tobacco parcels mentioned above, individuals could send one book parcel per month to a POW. However, the parcel with a maximum weight of 2.25kg, had to be dispatched from a publisher or bookseller to the censorship office in Oxford before onward dispatch to the POW camp.

All books were censored twice. First of all by the Allied power to ensure that no book could conceivably help the enemy. Secondly, by the German authorities to ensure that no book could possibly help in any attempts at escape or other subversive activity. All books by communist or Jewish writers were automatically banned. The inconsistency of censorship, on both sides, meant that some books that should have been censored got through the process and other books that were really quite innocuous were censored. According to the POW librarian in Stalag Oflag V11B at Eichstatt, Major Elliot Viney " there were usually ways of evading censorship. The only banned book we never succeeded in obtaining was the most curious of all – the English translation of Mein Kampf"

 Mac even learnt a bit more German. Years later (2004) he was having a beer with me in a pub near Cambridge. We started talking to a young couple in their twenties and the fellow turned out to be German. My father said a few German words and was complimented. He was asked where he learnt his language, "In a German prisoner of war camp", he replied.

Isn't he Sweet? In his playfulness

Churchill: "Never was the alliance of the allies closer and more effective as at present"

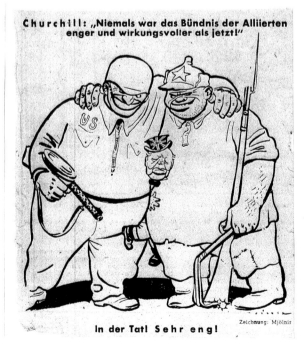

Indeed. Very narrow!

Apart from an enormous amount of reading to while away the monotony, my father collected some German 'cartoons' from newspapers. A selection is shown with appropriate translations. They are all undated but nevertheless give indications of the war from a German viewpoint (cartoonist/ propagandist)

It would seem that not every POW was unhappy with his lot. There is a story of a POW in another camp (Szchubin) told by Bill Armitage (in the book – The War Behind the Wire) where the POW " clearly enjoyed it and hoped the war would go on. He loved it for two reasons. Firstly, he could play bridge every afternoon for hours and secondly, because he never saw his wife. He thought it was a wonderful life"

My father wrote to his family in Northern Ireland and Marjorie Worrell in Northwich. All letters were censored but the gist of the letters painted a picture that things weren't too bad. Reassurance that he was alive and reasonably well. Mail was also received on an intermittent basis from family and friends. One very kind letter was received from Ian MacKenzie's mother, Mrs. Alice MacKenzie, from Brisbane, Australia. The letter was dated 19th November, 1944

Dear Mr. McIlroy,

I cannot say how very pleased I was to get your letter. I feel sure that every member of Ian's crew feels his death very much and we all appreciate the sympathy and good fellowship that existed amongst you all. It is very gratifying to know that he did his part nobly, though hard to know that he will never return. Through Con O'Connell we got a certain amount of information including his burial place, but would be more than delighted to welcome any of the crew in the future, and get all the information first hand.

I was sorry to hear recently that Con's father had died some months back. I wrote him (Con) some months ago, but doubt if he ever got it, neither have I heard from him direct, though I believe he wrote me, but I will write him again soon.

I will be pleased to hear from you again, and hope it won't be too long before you get home. Mr. MacKenzie joins me in wishing you a speedy return, also Heather (Ian's sister) (19) and Roy (17) are looking forward to meeting you one day. Kind regards,

Not many letters were as moving as this one, but the arrival of mail was generally a morale booster.

My father had written a 'thank you' postcard to the Caterpillar Club on 7 March 1944, receiving a reply in June 1944, as follows:

Dear Mr McIlroy,

Many thanks for your postcard of March 7th, and I am indeed glad that you were able to save your life with one of our chutes, although you were severely injured, and sincerely trust that you have now completely recovered.

I have much pleasure in welcoming you as a member of the Club, and in sending your membership card herewith, with our best wishes.

I regret that due to supply restrictions we shall not be able to obtain your Caterpillar until after the War but when you have a card to spare we shall be glad to have your home address so that I can send your Pin there as soon as available.

Yours sincerely,

Sec to L. Irvin

The camp shows were also a very important part of POW life. His scrap book records under 'Belaria Entertainments' the following.

"In our camp we have an excellent theatre built by POWs capable of seating 150 men fairly comfortably where we are entertained regularly, by classical gramophone records, amusing lectures of life in Australia, Canada and Argentina, talks on the CID, deep sea fishing, photography and a large variety of other interesting subjects."

I think the most enjoyable and by far the most popular entertainment held in the theatre are band shows, film, shows and plays. The latter entail a large amount of work in the form of stage construction, production and rehearsals all of which are performed by a few gifted POWs to whom we shall always be indebted for their continual services in keeping us amused and diverted during our otherwise monotonous stay in captivity. (The Geneva Convention 1929, Relative to the Treatment of Prisoners of War, mentions that the captor should make 'adequate provision for intellectual activity'. The German Camp authorities provided certain facilities to enable plays to be staged)

One evening programme was:

"Moonlight Serenade"	Band
"Alexander's Ragtime Band"	Band
"A Pretty Girl is like a Melody"	Arthur Darlow
"Piano Selections from Chopin"	Jack Normandalo
"A Selection of Popular Songs"	Bob Wagstaff
"Sophisticated Lady"	Band
"Some American Humour"	Jack Rose
"Brazil"	Jack Ross
"St Louis Blues"	Band

Interval

"Anvil Chorus"	Band
"Black Magic"	Johnny Kennedy
"Accordian Solo"	Reg Ryder
"Royal Garden Blues"	Octet
"Tea for Two"	Speciality Act
"Mexican Hat Dance"	Band
"Some English Humour"	Phil Jacobs
"Smoke gets in your eyes"	Arthur Darlow
"Siboney"	Jack Ross
" Signature Tune"	Band

Plays-shows seen while in captivity are listed in Appendix 13

A programme for one such show is:

BELARIA THEATRE

presents

"BANDWAGON"

Al Langille	Jack Ross
Arthur Darlow	Reg Ryder

Phil Jacobas	Bob Wagstaff
Johnny Kennedy	Jack Normandalo

Supported by

The Belaria Dance Orchestra

The Swingtime Octet

presented and conducted by

Leonard Whitely

Theatre Manager

B G Meharg

Electricians	Stage Management
J Pestridge	Freddy Allen
J Mansell	Tony Mays
	Cobber Fawcett &
	Bill Gillespie

There is a story of one aircrew officer arriving at the camp who said he had a ticket for 'Arsenic and Old Lace', being staged in London. He saw the Sagan Production instead, in late May 1944. Creative and artistic talent was not confined to these activities. There were a considerable number of men who provided services to various escape bids. There were tailors, map makers, forgers of various permits and passes, printers, engineers, tunnel diggers, equipment makers and so on. A modern day enterprise zone. There was also a poet, F/Lt WR Lott. He was in room 4-15 and wrote a verse for all the residents of 4-15. (Meharg's Mansion).

In the centre of the camp lies Meharg's Manse

Where we were thrown together by circumstance

Twelve different types in a crowded room

All Stalag conscious, but free from gloom

In four fifteen in four fifteen

Spelt four one five with a stroke between

A lusty bunch of bods contrive

To more or less remain alive

Take Joe mark one, he's bags of fun

His comic sayings take the bun

We can rely on him twice nightly

To burble forth "well I don't rightly...."

Presenting you Joe number two

A member of my own gen crew

Be it pudding or be it hash

His strident voice cries "Any gash?"

Chief chef is Reg, he's got the edge

On chow, from cake to soup and veg

When Reggie's lunches you have eaten,

You'll never sigh for Mrs Beaton

Griff could be billed as Actress(" skilled")

In plays where everyone gets killed

He looks so sweet in swishing skirts; he

Oughtn't to bow,he ought to curtesy

My pilot Frank once drove a Lanc

A Junkers filled it full of shank

In his three weeks he's heard the call

Of French fruit, springs and Volley Ball

"APPELL" OR ROLL CALL, WHEN, TWICE DAILY, WE WERE COUNTED BY THE GERMAN OFFICER IN CHARGE OF THE CAMP.

Boogie Woogie that's for Poogie

What else will rhyme but Flat Foot Floogie

Throw a ball - you find him leaping

Sound Appelle – you'll find him sleeping

Maurice W will not trouble you

But if you want his blood to bubble you

Natter to him nit-wit fashion

Before he's had his breakfast ration

Sheet metal worker, never a shirker

Is tin basher Les our klim tin jerker

His Spit is missing from the hanger

But he's aces with a wooden pranger

To Johnny now please make your bow

You wont? Well, shake hands anyhow

He studies law, that's no disgrace

Why should they call him "Bender Brace?"

Latest addition and bridge tactician

Is Don our Canadian proposition

When tricks are low and time is pressing

He'll slip in some pretty smart finessing

Peppered with flak we find old Mac

It's a marvel he wasn't swept into a sack

But "Mac" came over from County Down

Dead Irishmen simply wont lie down

Well that's the lot, I trust you've got

A fair idea of what is what,

I hope you've not been bored unduly

Thank you for listening - Yours very truly

When Bill Lott wrote these verses sometime in September 1944, room 4-15 had twelve residents. Geoff Evans had been repatriated and five new boys had arrived. F/Lt Bill Lott was a Bomb Aimer with 625 Squadron, flying Lancasters from RAF Kelstern. He was shot down on 29th July, 1944 and the plane crashed in the vicinity of Esslingen, on a mission to Stuttgart. He was captured on 5th August and interrogated by the Gestapo at Mussingen, near Stuttgart. Fortunately all his crew survived. Bill's pilot, F/O Frank Collett and navigator, F/O Joe Stephenson (Joe No 2) became residents of 4-15.

The other two new arrivals were F/O Viv Hobbs (Poogie) and F/Lt Don Belyea. Poogie was a Rhodesian from Bulawayo. He was a Lancaster pilot with 44 Squadron (Rhodesia) based at RAF Dunholme Lodge and was shot down on 29th May near the railway yards, Amiens, northern France. Two other crew members survived. F/Lt Don Belyea was a Canadian Lancaster pilot with 115 Squadron based at RAF Witchford. He was shot down on 13th August, 1944 on a mission to Braunschweig and was the only survivor of his crew.

June 1944 was a very significant month for the eight of them in 4-15 at the time and, of course, for the rest of the camp and all POWs everywhere. Secret radios (canaries) within the various constituent camps had picked up the faint voice of a BBC announcer John Snagge, from London. "D Day has come. Early morning (6 June) the Allies began the assault on the North Western face of Hitler's European Fortress". The Normandy landings had commenced. Word went round like wildfire. There was concern that discipline would break down, but the invasion was announced over the camp loudspeakers. The Germans had full confidence that the allied forces would be repulsed back into the sea but POW morale soared. And new prisoners arriving, when pressed for information, confirmed of large convoys, restricted areas around all Southern English ports, huge preparations and supply depots and massive troop concentration in South East England.

The start of the invasion raised their hopes that they might be home for Christmas; Four members of 4-15, Frank Collett, Paddy McIlroy, Johnny Brace and Bill Lott placed a wager with Don Belyea that the war would be over by 15th November, 1944. The wager was made in late August and consisted of wagering a 'D' bar each. This was an American chocolate/energy bar. In view of the food shortages, it was a very high wager. Needless to say, the four of them lost their bet and Don received four bars on the 15th November. In true service fashion, the transaction was noted as taking place at 23.50 hours.

In spite of the invasion, Mac and others were allowed to leave prison on parole for short periods.

A copy of a parole card:

PAROLE

I give my parole as a British Officer that on every occasion I use new sports field to the West of this Camp or go for a walk I will NOT

1.   Attempt to escape
2.   Make any preparations for future escapes
3.   Have any dealings with other persons outside the fences.

This card is strictly personal and I understand that any misuse will be considered as an infringement of my parole.

Mac's own parole walks were:

15 July 1944	Collected applies and fruit	1hr 15min
27 July 1944	Lovely weather - gathered fruit	1hr 45min
2 Aug 1944	Extremely hot - cool in the woods	2hr 5min
9 Aug 1944	Learned conditions in NCO's Camps from W/O	2hr 15min
17 Aug 1944	Not allowed to walk through fields or gather fruit due to the farmers objections	1hr 55min
30 Aug 1944	Excellent walk through the quiet and charming village of Eckersdorf - beautiful countryside	2hr 5min
6 Sept 1944	Through the village of Eckersdorf - very warm	2hr 30min

22 Sept 1944	Early morning - through Sagan and Eckersdorf	2hr 0min
25 Sept 1944	Extremely cold - excellent walk	3hr 15min
7 Oct 1944	Pleasant amble	2hr 0min

R.A.F. OFFICER PRISONERS OF WAR ASSEMBLING FOR COUNTING ON A WINTER MORNING.

As noted from his parole walks, the cold weather in September 1944 presaged a cold winter ahead. They weren't disappointed. Bill Lott wrote, in October, 1944, more poetry (A Kriegie Lament) in which one verse refers to the winter weather. The poem itself conveys a brilliant insight into the "British" sense of humour, and defiance, under such adverse conditions.

THE LAMENT

Here we are at Stalag Luft Three, drinking at the bar,

With lovely girls to buy us beer,

Like bloody hell, we are!

We travelled here in luxury, the whole trip for a quid,

A sleeping-berth for each of us,

Like bloody hell, we did!

Our feather-beds are two foot deep, the carpets almost new,

In easy chairs we lounge all day,

Like bloody hell, we do!

The Goons are really wizard chaps, their hopes of victory, good,

We'd change them places any day,

Like bloody hell, we would!

When winter comes and snow's around, the temperature at Nil,

We'll find six blankets on our beds,

Like bloody hell, we will!

It's heaven on earth at Stalag Three, a life we'd hate to miss,

It's everything we've always wished,

Like bloody hell, it is!

And when this war is over, and Jerry gets his bill,

We'll remember all that's happened here,

My bloody oath, we will!

About Christmas, 6 inches of snow fell. It was extremely cold and the home-made decorations in their huts and carol singing   helped to create as festive an atmosphere as possible. BUT why weren't they at home? However, they made the best of it. My father's scrap book recorded the following:

'Xmas Cooking, Room 13, Block 17, Belaria, Germany'

Apart from cookies and pies, the following Xmas cake was made by F/Lt Foster, RNZAF and F/Lt Collins, RAF, using the following ingredients:

4 bowls ground biscuit, 1 bowl bread crumbs, 1 ½ bowls of potatoes, 3 bowls of raisins, 4 carrots,

2 tins of margarine, 1 ½ of klim, 2 ½ of rolled oats, 1 klim tin of baking powder, 12 tablespoons of sugar, 3 tablespoons of syrup, 1 tablespoon of cinnamon, made in three layers.

Icing for the first layer (coffee) – klim sugar, biscuit and coffee

Second layer – chocolate icing

Third layer – margarine, honey, klim, biscuit, flour, sugar.

The entire cake with klim, margarine and sugar icing.

A marvellous Xmas pudding was made by F/Lt Foster, RNZAF and First LT Shostock, USAAF. This pudding was steamed for 24 hours before serving.

Father's scrap book continues;

We were issued with 2/3 parcel each on 23rd December, 1944 which enabled us to spend a very satisfactory Christmas. Our Christmas dinner was a very memorable occasion where everyone was on their best behaviour; speeches were made by several members of the mess under the able chairmanship of F/Lt Hugh Gillett. The most moving and I think the most suitable was given by First Lieutenant Walter Shostack (from Dayton, Ohio) of the United States Army Air Force, who finished up with the Lords Prayer, which I think reminded us all of the dear Lord whose birthday we were celebrating, a thing most of us are inclined to forget. The meal took place under conditions which conformed and compared favourably to those of an Officers' mess.

At this time, camp and German sources informed the POWs that the Russian army was heading westwards, in their direction, seemingly faster than the allied forces from the west. Where would we spend next Christmas?

They were propelled by rumours. Rumours that as the allies (Russians) approached, the camp as others in the East, would be overrun by the Russians and liberated. Or the Russians would take them prisoner and their fate would be in Russian hands. Or the Russians would arm them and compel them to fight the Germans. Or the Germans would kill them all before making their preparations for the final defence of the Fatherland. Or the Germans would use them as hostages for bargaining purposes. Liberation from the camp meant many things. In mid January 1945, in the coldest German winter for 50 years, a new batch of Red Cross parcels was received, and fully distributed amongst the POWs. None were kept back. They were advised by Senior RAF Officers to get as fit as possible. Nobody really knew what was going to happen, including the German camp guards.

During January, 1945, rumours abounded that the Russians were massing on the River Oder. 30 kilometres east of our camp. The 'scrap book' continues:

Hopes were raised again that we might soon be liberated. This was not to be. The Germans decided to evacuate our camp (Belaria) and march us deeper into Germany. At 9.30 on the evening of the 27th January, the camp was given 30 minutes to prepare to leave. In fact, departure from Belaria was delayed. American POWs were evacuated from the South and West compounds and in the early hours of the 28th January, British and Commonwealth POWs left the North, East and Centre compounds. A final parade took place, in Belaria, in darkness on the 28th January (just after midnight) The delay was fortunate because it enabled POWs to better prepare for the ordeal ahead. Quite a number of sledges were constructed from bed boards, coal boxes, Red Cross boxes and various bits of furniture, so more food and clothing could be taken.

I took what I could carry, including my 'scrap book' and wore as many layers of clothes as I could. I also stuffed newspapers inside my great coat for extra protection against the bitter cold. Food was the priority and each prisoner was given a Red Cross parcel (which may have been the last for all we knew) as we marched out of the camp into temperatures ranging between 20-30 degrees below zero. There was thick snow on the ground. It was dark and freezing. The evacuation commenced around 4 am and it must have taken quite a few hours for the camp to empty. In the still of night, gunfire could be heard. German, Russian… we couldn't tell.

ON THE MARCH

CHAPTER 7

THE MARCH TO LUCKENWALDE AND ESCAPE

POWs were warned that stragglers would at best be left to die; they may be shot. Mac understood that about 10% of them failed to make the journey. They were ill prepared for marching (after all, they were aircrew) inadequate clothing and boots, generally unfit, and half starved before the event, but were each handed a Red Cross parcel as they left the camp.

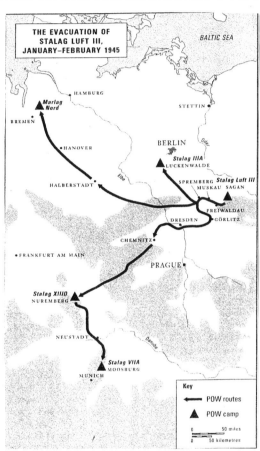

4. Evacuation of Stalag Luft 3, Jan 1945

My father's notes record the following:

Prodded by German guns, about 10,000 of us left Sagan, the East, West, North, South and Centre compounds, and Belaria (of which about 2000 from Belaria) wearing an assortment of clothing and carrying odd bundles (or pulling sledges) of whatever kit we could. The line of POWs threaded its way through the German countryside for about 12 miles to the small village of Lennier, near Kunau. By the time the last man had left the camp, the first party to leave were near and around Kunau. 12 miles of misery. The column was 'guarded' by Volksturmers. These were elderly men in their 'sixties' who did not want the job and were as ignorant as we were. Nobody knew where we were going, except perhaps the very few Luftwaffe officers who were in overall control.

It was a battle to survive as we plodded through the adverse elements of snow, ice, and blizzards. Conditions were truly arctic. On arrival we were put into barns. The 'accommodation' was unheated and in some cases open to the elements which allowed ingress of snow. After bagging a bit of space, very modest meals were cooked over small fires and hot drinks brewed. It was very cold and we were advised to remove our boots at night and dry our socks under our arms or between our legs to prevent them being frozen in the morning. Fresh snow would fall during the night.

We weren't the only group on the roads. Refugees were heading west, trying to keep ahead of the Russian advance. Foreign workers were being marched from camps in the East. German military and civilians were as frightened as us. Perhaps more so. The Russians had a lot of unfinished business to attend to. And the Germans knew it.

The following day, 29th January, the POWs left Kunau and marched to Gross Selten. The 'accommodation' here was better. The barns had more straw.

Mac's notes continue; The next day, we were on parade around 9.30 am to be counted and prepare for the day's journey. We were very pleased to be told that we were staying put for the day. And none of the rumours flying around could be confirmed or denied. On the 31st January we marched another 18 miles to Tschopfelen, near Birkenstadt. Conditions changed in the afternoon as a thaw set in. Sledging became more difficult and so more kit and supplies had to be carried. The 'accommodation' was an unheated barn with no light. A barn nearby had electricity, running water and heating and was home for a herd of dairy cows.

The POWs remained in the Birkenstadt area, in various hamlets and villages, for another day. At the end of this day (our fifth) we were given a fifth of a loaf each; this was the first and only food given to us by the Germans during the march.

THE BARN AT BIRKENSTADT

On the 2nd February we marched through slush and mud to Graustein, near Schonheide and another night in another cold barn. The following day we marched to Spremberg where the various columns of POWs were divided. The American POWs headed south west in the direction of Munich, where the majority were liberated by US Forces. In the afternoon we were temporarily locked up in empty sheds in a large German Tank Corps depot before marching to the railway station to begin our train journey to Luckenwalde. Here we were stuffed into and locked in cattle trucks, 50-60 men per truck. Conditions were truly dreadful. We took it in turns to stand up, sit and lie down. Quite a number of men had dysentery and in those cramped conditions a bucket was passed round, sometimes over our heads. It was emptied whenever the train stopped, which was frequently, and the doors opened. Nobody was allowed off. Twenty four hours later the train arrived at Luckenwalde, south of Berlin.

The journey had been unpleasant, disgusting and humiliating. During this journey a German Foreign Office official asked the Senior British Officer on board for a statement that the Germans had endeavoured to improve conditions and acted properly at all times. The British Officer refused.

On arrival the POWs detrained and marched in pouring rain from the station to the gates of the camp. There was a ninety minute delay before entry to the camp. The camp was in total darkness as the air raid sirens had gone off.

Every prisoner had to be deloused, cold showered and searched before entry. They were counted 4 times, each count being different, before entry into the camp. They were cold, tired, hungry, sick, frightened and feeling pretty miserable. How most of them survived that terrible journey and experience is a mystery. The human mind and body seems to be able to take a great deal of punishment: sheer mental and physical determination can overcome the odds. Mac's damaged right leg was very painful from time to time, but somehow it got him there.

Mac's notes continue:

The camp proved to be a dreadfully dirty place, swarming with rats. They were everywhere even in what passed as a loo. This was a shed of some sort; three walls were each lined with 5 open loos - a total of 15. There was no privacy and no flushing system, and they had not been emptied for months, or perhaps even years. According to Bill Lott, compared to Luckenwalde, Belaria was a five star hotel.

It got worse as more prisoners arrived. The later arrivals, many American, were put in tents or marquees. We were accommodated in 3 tier bunks, cheek by jowl. I had the top one, Ted and Eric who became my new friends had the other two. I had lost touch with my old friends from Hut 4-15, and only saw one of them again. (Bill Lott, in the 1960s) I did not see any members of my crew again.

Apart from the increasingly dreadful conditions, we were getting even hungrier. Rations were cut. A loaf of bread was divided into six or seven to last all day. Each man was given some soup and potatoes, and very small quality of margarine and cheese. Mint tea or acorn coffee was distributed twice a day. And there was nothing much to do at Luckenwalde. Hours and hours were spent sitting about doing nothing, not even reading. There were no books, no camp library, and no mail. Everyone, including the guards was waiting for something good to happen.

Outside the confines of the camp the war was beginning to reach its climax. The Russian forces had over run East Prussia and Allied forces occupied German territory in the west. There was a fear that once battles took place on German soil the fighting would be intense and stubborn. It was clear that Allied losses were to be minimised in the final stages of the conflict, at the expense of the Germans. The use of air power, as the 'long range artillery' was therefore the key to a decisive victory, so the selection of targets by the Joint Chiefs of Staff and heads of the Russian, British and American governments was fully justified by the military situation at the time.

5. Greater Germany, 1st Jan 1945

The map of "Greater Germany" in January, 1945 shows not only, at this stage of the war, that original borders of Germany remained, but that they occupied Northern Italy, Yugoslavia, Austria, Czechoslovakia, parts of Hungary, Holland, Denmark and Poland. Within this large geographical area hundreds of thousands of prisoners and slave workers were at the mercy of the German forces and Nazi regime.

It is extraordinary to note that some of the actions of Bomber Command and the US Air Force during this crucial and critical time were being subject to intense political scrutiny and criticism. Some politicians were beginning to feather their post war political nests, particularly after the bombing of Dresden on 13/14th February. Dresden and Berlin were both considered "transportation and industrial areas" Many Dresden factories produced war materials. The Zeiss-Ikon camera factory produced gun sights. A cigarette manufacturer produced ammunition. It will be observed that geographically Dresden was in the centre of "Greater Germany" excluding Italy and Yugoslavia. The output of its factories and its intact transport links, to ferry equipment and personnel remained a threat to all Allied forces.

The continuation of bombing was essential. The Germans had also been developing "secret" weapons whose deployment may well have altered the course of the war. Albert Speer notes that development of a ground to air missile had been completed in 1942, under the code name "Waterfall". This rocket was "capable of carrying approximately 660 pounds of explosives along a directional beam up to an altitude of 50000 feet and hitting enemy bombers with great accuracy. It was not affected by day or night, by clouds or fog" He considered that this "rocket, in conjunction with the new ME 262 jet fighters would have beaten back the western allies air offensive" Considered by his peer group to be the most outstanding test pilot, Captain Eric "Winkle" Brown, CBE, DSC, AFC, RN in his book "Wings on my Sleeve" was of the opinion that the ME 262 was the most formidable aircraft of World War 2. Captain Brown flew an ME 262 after hostilities had ceased in 1945. Apart from its armament of 4 30mm cannon which could be supplemented with 48 air to air missiles, 24 under each wing, the aircraft was at least 100 mph faster than any other and could therefore 'dictate its own combat terms'.

Speer also states that "on 14th October, 1942 a (second) rocket had successfully flown the prescribed course of one hundred and twenty miles and had struck within two and a half miles of the target. For the first time a product of man's inventive mind had grazed the frontiers of space at an altitude of sixty miles". The first V1 flying bomb (V – Vergeltungswaffe – revenge weapon) was fired on London on 13th June, 1944, a week after the Normandy landings. The objective of the Third Reich was that the bombardment would force the British government to negotiate. 10632 V1s were launched against London and the Home Counties (from northern France) between 13th June and 5th September. Nearly 53% exploded in the targeted area. With the loss of launch sites between Cherbourg and St. Omer, after the D-Day landings, the Luftwaffe adapted over 100 Heinkel 111 Bombers to launch, from under the port wing, V1 rockets. About 1400 were launched in this way in the 4 months to 14th January, 1945, of which 21% landed in the target area. Over 6800 people perished and nearly 18000 were injured from V1 attacks on England.

The V2 rocket offensive against England commenced on 8th September, 1944 and finished on 27th March, 1945. 1269 missiles were launched of which 87% landed in the intended area. 2724 people lost their lives. Perhaps the politicians making the most noises about Dresden should have gone to Farringdon Market, London after a V2 attack in March, 1945 killed 300 civilians. In mainland Europe, 1739 V-2 missiles were launched against cities in Holland, Belgium and France, causing 7000 deaths.

In retaliation to the bombing of Dresden, the use of poisonous gases in warheads was discussed at the highest levels. Germany had vast stocks of Tabun and Sarin. A 250kg Sarin bomb was considered likely to destroy all life within several square kilometres of the exposure point. These gas warheads were not employed, for fear of counter retaliation. Of greater significance was the testing of a 'small atom bomb' on the 11th October, 1944 on the Baltic island of Rugen, not far from Peenemunde. Geoffrey Brooks states that "if there ever was such a thing (test) Hitler's scientists had won the race to the atom bomb"

What would have happened to my father and hundreds of thousands in similar circumstances if such weapons had been deployed en masse? According to opinions in his memoirs, Eisenhower considered "that if the A-4 (V-2) had been operational six months earlier it would have made the invasion extremely difficult if not impossible" One can only speculate what would have happened to the millions of people on German territory.

As regards the bombing of German cities Air Marshall Harris, in a reply to Air Marshall Norman Bottomley on the 29th March, stated that "attacks on cities like any other act of war are intolerable unless they are strategically justified. But they are strategically justified in so far as they shorten the war and so preserve the lives of allied soldiers. To my mind we have absolutely no right to give them up unless it is certain that they will not have this effect. I do not personally regard the whole of the remaining cities of Germany as worth the bones of one British Grenadier"

Fortunately, for my father and thousands of others, the war was drawing to a close although they couldn't be sure of this at the time. There were still, however, a few more dramas to endure. Mac's notes continue:

On April 14, as the Russian Army approached, it was decided that we would be moved to Munich. Accordingly we were marched, at gunpoint, to the railway station, and once again stuffed into and locked in cattle trucks which we had come to know (but not love) so well. We were told that we would be off as soon as an engine was found. The engine failed to appear so the following evening we marched back to camp with the usual palaver of counting and recounting us.

All the time, rumours were flying around. Even the German guards did not know what was going on. In a different way they were suffering almost as much as them. One strong rumour was that the POWs were going to be used as hostages. Berlin was a possible destination. Another rumour was that of massacre. Another that the Russians, once they overran the camps, would enlist us to fight for the Russian Army, as the Russians did for all Russian POWs, however fit they were.

6. The Advance of the Red Army, 1945

The sound of intense bombardment in the third week of April heralded the closely approaching Russians. The POWs were 'entertained' by aerial dogfights and cannon shells rattling on our tin roof and dropping around us. On the 21 April they assembled for the normal morning roll call, and at mid-morning, the German guards and camp staff lined up on parade on the road through the camp and marched off westwards. As soon as they left the camp they discarded their uniforms and put on civilian clothes. The POWs lined the barbed wire fences and cheered them off.

The camp was now in 'no mans land'. The camp's previously prepared Defence Scheme was put into operation. Men were allocated to defence and guard post duties. They wore a white arm band with a green cross. The duties were non-combatant and apart from Russian POWs, who were expected to fight the Germans at every opportunity, all nationalities participated. Patrols were sent out to establish the whereabouts of the Russian army and white flags were placed on watchtowers. A large POW sign was laid in the compound to warn aircraft of the camp's status. The principle objective was to ensure as much as possible the orderly running of the camp. Various repairs were carried out. The telephone system, which the Germans damaged before leaving the camp, was repaired. German radio sets were retrieved from their "compound" and distributed around the camp. A quantity of arms and ammunition was found and stored securely.

Refugees arrived at the camp but the (POW) guards had instructions to refuse admittance. Some German soldiers arrived and surrendered. The best part of 20,000 people was anxiously awaiting their fate.

The detailed diary notes of Alex Ager record some of the events of that day (21 April)

1935 hours: Two independent German and Russian sources reported Russian artillery

At Waltersdorf, 2.5 miles NE of Luckenwalde, to be shelling the town.

2100 hours: It was reported that only about 1000 Volksturm and Hitler Youth, both armed with Tommy guns, rifles and Panzerfausts are defending Luckenwalde. Several buildings and factories are ablaze in the town which was bombed by Russian aircraft this afternoon. Rumours say that Russian and American forces have linked up in TREBBIN, 8 miles away to north.

2230 hours: Fires were seen WSW and W of the camp, the latter probably indicating fighting at TREUENBRITZEN, 14 miles away.

Alex's notes continue, starting with events at 0030 hours, Sunday, 22nd April

A delegation from the ex-mayor of Luckenwalde visited the camp offering to hand over the town to the camp authorities for subsequent surrender to the Russian army.

(The offer was refused by General Ruge, the senior Allied officer)

The delegation stated that the Volksturm units had been disbanded and that there were no German troops left.

0600 hours: The first Russian armoured cars entered the camp and left 30 minutes later taking General Ruge (a Norwegian general) to Luckenwalde. Owing to being fired upon, the American senior officer and an interpreter, who were riding on the outside of the armoured car ended their journey rapidly (they jumped into a ditch and made their way back to camp)

My father's notes continue:

On the morning of 22 April, T34 Russian tanks of the First Ukrainian Army arrived and just charged through the barbed wire and the main camp gates were smashed aside, followed by a dozen lorries, full of soldiers. The Russians were a young, ragged lot indeed, even dirtier and scruffier than we were. They looked tough and were heavily armed. We cheered them as they drove down the central road of the camp. Two German fighter planes flew over the camp, strafing it, and machine guns and small arms fire could be heard from the nearby woods.

The Russians stopped for a while for refreshment, rounded up and armed as many Russian POW's as possible and marched them to join the fight. About 20% of the POWs (4,000) were Russian.

Within two hours they had sped off, smashing through the barbed wire, after the retreating Germans.

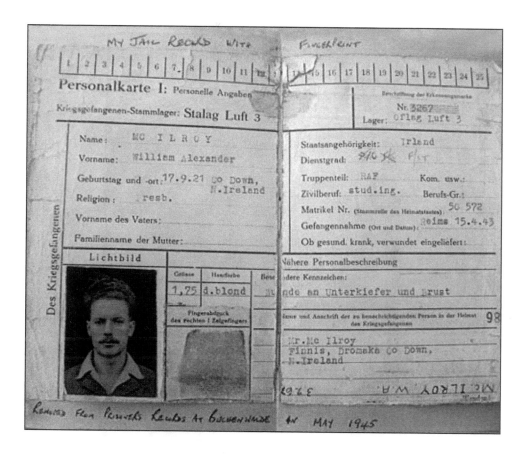

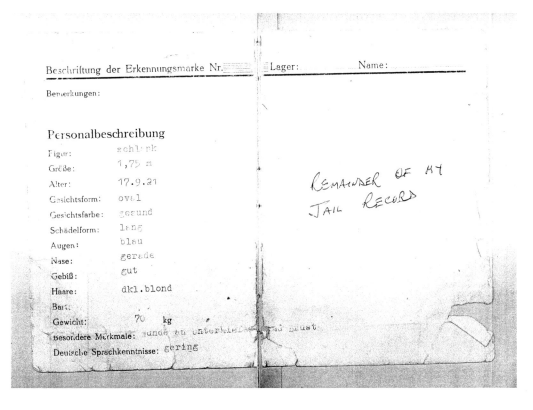

We had a taste of freedom for a short while, although we were instructed not to leave the camp. I used this period to break into the camp administration office and remove my jail records. A foraging party was sent out to collect food and they also stole 6 rifles from an SS unit in the woods nearby. When the Unit Commander became aware of this, he stormed into the camp and threatened to open fire on the camp if the rifles were not produced immediately. Needless to say they were.

Apart from some minor resistance the town of Luckenwalde was quickly and efficiently occupied. Alex Ager noted that two independent and reliable witnesses stated that the discipline and behaviour of the Russian troops, to the astonishment of the Germans, was correct in every way. By 1100 hours (22nd April) most of the Russian troops had left the town and the German civilians began looting the shops, breaking all shop windows and taking footwear and linen goods. One hotel was also looted. White flags were flying everywhere and the civilians were asking "where are the Americans?" In the afternoon the only Russians in the town were traffic controllers and guards at key points.

At 2100 hours one officer returning from the town reported everything quiet and orderly early in the evening, but later there was quite a lot of firing and patrols were out on the streets. On the way down to the town that evening a party of Russian ex-POWs from this camp was ambushed by German civilians and 4 Russians were killed. The German civilians were subsequently captured. Firing continued during the night to the north where German groups were still resisting. The NE part of Luckenwalde was shelled by German artillery.

At 2345 hours, 2 German soldiers surrendered to one of our patrols. 30 minutes later 6 more soldiers (from the Friedrich Ludwig Jahn) surrendered to another of our officers. They were all arrested and handed over to the Russian Military Authorities.

Alex's diary captures the volatility, danger, uncertainty and tensions of this time.

My father's notes continue:

'A few days later, 25 April, the follow up Russian administrators arrived. They were an older, cleaner lot, and immediately gave us instructions to repair the barbed wire fencing. Watch towers were manned by Russian guards. Armed guards were positioned at 50 yard intervals around the camp perimeter, and another cordon was established 2 miles away. We found out later that Cossacks, on horseback, with rifles and sabres had been patrolling in the vicinity of the camp, particularly the wooded areas. Perimeter patrols restarted. POWs were warned not to think of leaving the camp. This was probably sensible as fighting was still raging nearby. The POWs found outside the wire were recaptured and returned inside at gunpoint. After a few days "freedom", they were POWs again. With a different jailer'

Apparently Stalin had ordered that American and British prisoners were not to be released until promises were obtained from Roosevelt and Churchill that all Russian POWs who had fought for the Germans would be returned to Russia. This was a part of the Yalta Agreement 1945 which none of the POWs had ever heard of. Stalin's political agenda was also linked to his requirement for full control of Poland. This is indeed an irony. The failure of German forces to withdraw from Poland in 1939 caused Great Britain and France to declare war. In 1945, Poland had its second master in six years. The Russian plan was to move British and American POWs to the port of Odessa (Crimea) in the meantime, and then by sea to UK, or to Moscow and then by air. An estimated 500 British prisoners were held for months and eventually got back to England via Odessa.

Alex Ager's diary notes of the 28th April record the following details:

The first elements of the Russian Repatriation Staff have arrived in the camp.

Following a brief meeting with the Russian Captain in Charge, the Senior Allied Officer called a meeting of the Senior Officers of all nationalities of the camp to let them know such information as he had been able to obtain.

Captain Medvedev, the Russian Officer, belongs to the staff of General Famin and is bringing with him a convoy of 50 lorries which should arrive sometime tonight containing 100 tons of food and clothing as well as 50 pigs.

On his arrival this evening, Captain Medvedev was very tired, having been on the road for 5 days and did not wish to discuss details this evening. The Senior Allied Officer, however, managed to have a brief talk with him over a cup of coffee. His first interest was the convoy, which had been split up.

The Senior Allied Officer asked Captain Medvedev if he could say the probable date and route for the return home of the prisoners of this camp. Captain Medvedev said that the position of this camp is peculiar in that it is the first camp which his staff has ever had to repatriate from which the prisoners might be sent West. He said that, as Luckenwalde was still in an operational area, it was not certain which would be the quickest way to return us, via Odessa or the West, but he thought that whichever road or rail route became serviceable first, East or West, would be used. It appears that there are representatives of the Allied Nations attached to a permanent Repatriation Board in Moscow and full reports of the camp strength would be sent to them immediately. Captain Medvedev, when asked about Allied Liason Officers, said that he had never heard of them and as far as he was concerned, the date and route of the repatriation of the camp would be decided by the Russian Government, in contact with the International Repatriation Representatives. As soon as this question was settled, orders for evacuation would be issued to the prisoners of each nationality. He emphasised that there would be no march whatever route was decided upon. As Captain Medvedev was unable to give an official statement, the Senior Allied Officer asked him for his personal opinion but he refused to commit himself on either the route or date of repatriation.

The question of our return, he said, was now an international one and he himself, as a junior officer, was not in a position to quote exact details. His duty, while waiting for the roads to be cleared was to take charge of this camp and so organise it that each national group of prisoners was prepared ready to move. He told the Senior Allied Officer that each national group would move under separate arrangement.

Captain Medvedev has a staff of 15 officers, 200 other ranks and some 20 girls whose function is not quite clear-probably interpreters. The Captain's further responsibility was the issue of food and clothing as necessary. He said that W/Cdr Collard would still be required to be responsible as Senior Allied Officer for the whole Stalag, for a while at least. W/Cdr Collard said that he would naturally be glad to return to his duties concerned with purely British interests. Captain Medvedev said that he did not propose to deal directly with the camp Internal Administration but he would release W/Cdr Collard from his duties as Senior Allied Officer as soon as possible. The Senior Allied Officer told Captain Medvedev that the stores were ready to receive the 100 tons of food and clothing and interpreters were waiting to meet the lorries which began to arrive shortly after this was being written. Captain Medvedev is to discuss more detailed arrangements with the

S.A.O. tomorrow.

My father's notes continue:

This unwelcome delay in our release and the unwholesome prospect of being taken to Russia resulted in a great deal of frustration. There were rumours that the POWs would be transferred to another camp where conditions were supposedly better. The prospect of another march was appalling. It really was time to try and get out. Against the strict orders of the senior officers, my friends, Ted Haddock, from Durham and Eric Burdett, from Boscombe, Hampshire, and I, crawled under a damaged part of the barbed wire fence, at night, with other small parties. Avoiding detection we ran into the woods and laid low for a while. We then started to walk westwards along forest tracks, in complete darkness. During the day of the 4th May we heard sporadic small arms gunfire and were extremely anxious not to be recaptured by either the German or Russian forces. That would have been calamitous. Many were recaptured, but we managed to evade capture and reached the American front line, after 4 days, where we met up with a patrol of GIs on their way back to their quarters by the River Elbe. They hauled us on board a truck and took us straight to the American 9th Army cookhouse where there was a welcome sight of hot food - lots and lots of it. Although still in Germany, we were free at last. Food, showers, decent clean clothes, decent bed. We wandered around for the next few days experiencing sheer freedom. It was unreal. German army uniforms were discarded everywhere. I took a souvenir from a German tunic (JFM Schonebeck No87085). Bodies were seen floating down the Elbe. The local Germans were suddenly very friendly and indeed delighted that the Americans had arrived before the Russians. One family - mother, father and teenage daughter invited me to their home for tea. They live in a nice well furnished house and indeed didn't seem to have suffered at all during the war. What a difference it would have been if the Russians arrived first. We had a cup of tea and cake and as I left the daughter whispered to me "Iche liebe dich" - it was a strange experience and something of a shock to find that Germans could be friendly.

After a few more days and much eating, my father, and hundreds of others were taken by truck from Magdeburg to Hannover, a distance of about 85 miles. There was a "shuttle" service to Reims. He was stuffed with a great number of other POWs in an American military Dakota and flown from Hanover to their headquarters in Reims (11 May). The general surrender of German forces to General Montgomery had taken place 6 days before on Luneburg Heath. The following day, 12th May, Mac and other POWs were packed, 25 at a time, into every nook and cranny of a Lancaster bomber and flown to Oxford. The weather was cold but they still had to strip, get deloused and showered before entering the Officers Mess. His war and ordeal were over, at last. The war continued for 3 more days. The bulk of the prisoners in Stalag IIIA were not released until 20 May. They were loaded onto Russian trucks and deposited at the Elbe with the American 9th Army. Con O'Connell was released from Luckenwalde on 22nd May. It is assumed that the rest of the crew of JB 909 were released at or around this time.

Date	Hour	Aircraft Type and No.	Pilot	Duty	REMARKS (including results of bombing, gunnery, exercises, etc.)	Flying Times Day	Flying Times Night
		MAY 1945			MAY 1945	HRS MNS 1388.50	
					Time carried forward:—	221.10	
11.5.45	1100	DAKOTA	CAPTAIN CORBETT	PASSENGER	HANOVER - RHEIMS - (EVACUATION P.O.W. CAMP)	2.10	
12.5.45	1430	LANCASTER	F/LT SINCLAIR	- DO -	RHEIMS - OXFORD REPATRIATION FROM P.O.W. CAMP	1.50	
					DELOUSED TWICE AFTER INTERROGATION		
	EX P_____ of W__			DAKOTA LANCASTER	TOTAL FLYING HOURS HRS MNS 1392.50		
1.6.45			F/LT				
					TOTAL TIME ...		

Mac's Flying Log, May 1945

Although Mac's war was over, the form filling wasn't. The day after he landed at Oxford, from Reims, he had to complete and submit a form Appendix 'D', Annex 'C'.

"Post Hostilities Evacuation of Prisoners of War from Germany and the Continent".

Since RAF officers are responsible for the maintenance of their clothing and will have received Income Tax Relief in respect of the upkeep of their kit during the period of their captivity they will be required to make some payment for items of clothing received from public sources while in captivity or on route to repatriation.

The 'form' duly completed is shown in Appendix 5. POWs were all flabbergasted that within 24 hours of repatriation they were asked to do this. Mac didn't have much kit anyway. And much of it was left in his room at RAF Leeming, a room he 'vacated' two years before. As referred to earlier, some of it was 'borrowed', including private (civilian) clothing and shoes!

A day later Mac was interrogated about the aircraft loss, as referred to earlier. The other surviving crew members apart from two were interrogated on the 27/28th May. It is assumed they remained at Luckenwalde until released by the Russians. Canter, the second pilot who evaded capture, submitted his report earlier in June, 1943. The Canadian flight engineer. Lloyd McKenzie was a POW at Stalag Kopernikus and got back to England a few days before my father.

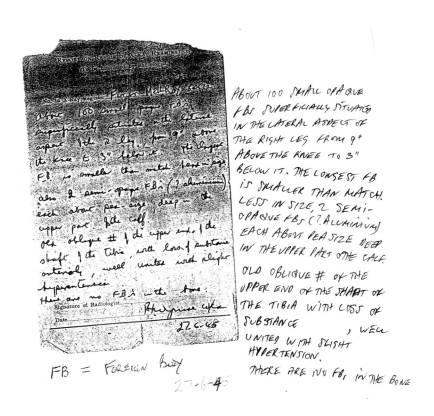

ABOUT 100 SMALL OPAQUE FBs SUPERFICIALLY SITUATED IN THE LATERAL ASPECT OF THE RIGHT LEG FROM 9" ABOVE THE KNEE TO 3" BELOW IT. THE LONGEST FB IS SMALLER THAN MATCH. LESS IN SIZE, 2 SEMI-OPAQUE FBs (? ALUMINIUM) EACH ABOUT PEA SIZE DEEP IN THE UPPER PART OTHE CALF.

OLD OBLIQUE # OF THE UPPER END OF THE SHAFT OF THE TIBIA WITH LOSS OF SUBSTANCE , WELL UNITED WITH SLIGHT HYPERTENSION. THERE ARE NO FB, IN THE BONE

FB = FOREIGN BODY
27-6-45

RADIOLOGIST REPORT 27th JUNE 1945

5 weeks later, Mac's right leg was x-rayed, and about 100 bits of shrapnel (foreign bodies) showed up on the Radiologist Report as shown. Fortunately, he did not have to fill in another form declaring these facts!   On the 17th May, 1945 he returned home to the farm in Dromara. Fresh eggs at last. At this time a letter was received by my grandparents from Madame Chatelin It was sent from 44, Boulevard Lundy, Reims and dated 7th May.

44, BOULEVARD LUNDY
REIMS . TÉLÉP. 59-21

7th of may 45

Dear Sir -
I am thinking of your son and of all the fine boys who have suffered in Germany, and of those who died there, this evening of all evenings, when we have heard that the armistice is signed. -
I hope your son is home near you now -
I shall be glad if you let me know. -
Thank God that the first part of this nightmare is over - at last ! - Your's Sincerely
J. Chatelin

Her letter sums up the relief that must have been felt all over Europe.

20. Mac, Back on the Farm, May 1945

21. VIP Crew with General Montgomery and a French Colonel, 1947

22. Jack Conan, Army Pilot, Austria, 1947

23. Mac, 1947

24. Ian MacKenzie's Memorial Unveiled by the Australian Ambassador, April 1955

25. Memorial, 2006

26. Street Name Plates

27. Madam Lefevre with JB 909 Propeller Blade

28. The Serial Plate of JB 909

29. Mac, Visiting MacKenzie's Memorial, May 2005

30. Mac with Madame Hebert, Daughter of Madam Chatelin, May 2005

31. Mac Visiting French Air Base BA 112 Museum, Reims with Jacques Pernet and Simon McIlroy (in the Background)

32. Mac Reunited with Alex Ager, January 2006

CHAPTER 8

VIENNA AND BEYOND

After hostilities had ceased, at least in Europe, the Armed Services began reducing manpower. Many service personnel couldn't wait to leave and return to Civvy Street. Understandable. Others wished to remain in the forces but were not required; this included many trained pilots and aircrew. My father had decisions to make; should he stay in or leave the RAF? British Overseas Airways Corporation (BOAC), the predecessor to British Airways had their pick of RAF pilots, especially from Bomber Command but they were actively seeking to recruit Wireless Operators. Mac was offered a position as a wireless operator with BOAC but decided to stay in the Royal Air Force and was accepted.

In October 1945, he was posted to 1383 TCU (Transport Conversion Unit) RAF Crosby on Eden, Carlisle, for further training, as a wireless operator, on Dakotas. During this time he also received training as a second pilot. In December he was assessed for W/T (wireless telegraphy) and radio assessment (liaison); his lowest mark was 82%, highest 96%. In mid January, 1946 he had a spot of leave in Cheshire, to visit my mother before returning to a new posting with 24 Squadron, RAF Hendon Transport Command in February. The crew seemed to spend a lot of time flying to RAF Bassingbourne, Cambridgeshire, all of 20 minutes each flight. In late February after 4 weeks at Hendon, the squadron was moved to Bassingbourne where the airfield was much larger; it was safer. Mac was based at Bassingbourne for five weeks, and then posted to Vienna as part of the personal aircrew of General Sir Richard McCreery flying Dakotas. General McCreery was the British High Commissioner in Vienna from July, 1945 to May, 1946. The Russian Army, approaching from Hungary, liberated the city of Vienna on 12th April, 1945, and on the 27th April, Austria was declared independent. A provisional federal government was established, under Russian sponsorship, under the veteran Social Democrat, Karl Renner.

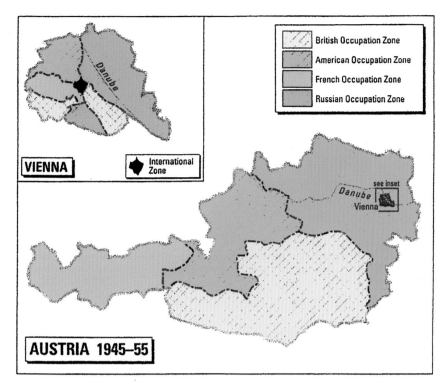

The country, which was restored to its 1937 geographical boundaries, was divided into four zones, each occupied by one of the victorious allied powers – USA, Britain, Russia and France. The city of Vienna, although in the Russian zone, was also divided into four zones but the centre itself, the Innere Stadt, was designated as an 'international' sector. This sector was controlled by the four Powers, on a rotating monthly basis and there was free movement between all zones, unlike Berlin.

Mac's new base was the 'Landing Strip' Vienna, where the Austrian Communications Flight was stationed. The crew flew the General, his staff and various VIPs to many different places in Europe and the Middle East including Iraq, Libya, Egypt, Sudan and Yemen. Destinations included Berlin and Hamburg, places my father certainly didn't expect to visit again. On 15th May, General Sir James Steele replaced General McCreery. The Dakota pilot was Flt.Lt Mack AFC, whose father was the British Ambassador in Vienna. Mack retired from the RAF in September and became a pilot with Pan American Airways. His replacement was Sqn Ldr Wainwright. In Vienna my father met an Army Captain, Jack Conan, who was a pilot and became a lifelong friend. Jack's job was to find suitable landing strips in Austria and especially around Vienna. When Mac was not on VIP duties Jack and he had many an interesting flight in Jack's Auster aircraft, looking for these landing sites, and quite often would land in a field where the grass was almost as high as the plane. The Auster was a 3/4 seater aircraft with a single engine of 130-150 h.p. It played a pioneering role in the formation of the Air Observation Post Squadrons in 1941. It was very versatile as Jack proved on all occasions and was capable of landing on quite small and uneven patches of land. After the war it was initially sold, for civilian purposes through car dealers! Mac was Jack's 'navigator' and quite often the pilot on these flights. The main landing strip in Vienna was in a built up area and required some really difficult manoeuvres in order to land. On one occasion, (31st May, 1946) while carrying out an air test they crash landed; this was my father's 5th plane crash. They ended up, the pair of them, sitting in their seats, on the ground, surrounded by the debris of the plane. However, within days Jack was allocated another Auster.

My father's initial accommodation in Vienna, was in the Officers Mess. This was an apartment of two floors, ground and first, in 16 Lainzer Strasse. He shared the mess with the Dakota navigator, Parkin and with Jack Conan. They survived very well. Parkin was a steady sort of chap, but Jack (from Southern Ireland) and my father (from Northern Ireland) would often have high spirited fights on the first floor balcony, and try to throw each other off. They referred to these skirmishes as the Battle of the Boyne, but luckily, neither of them did get thrown off the balcony. It was all highly dangerous as they could have killed each other but it didn't occur to them at the time. They were the best of friends! If things were a little quiet, my father would put a gramophone record on of 'Finlandia', on top volume. This incensed Jack so much that it actually ended up with another fight on the balcony! Jack could also be mischievous. On a number of occasions Jack would grab father's RAF hat and throw it out of the jeep, as they were driving rapidly through the streets of Vienna.

In keeping with RAF regulations they had a mess 'committee' to discuss issues of a 'service' nature. These regular meetings took less than 5 minutes. However, one meeting took 15 minutes. The three of them, Jack, Parkin and my father discussed how they could sell some surplus coffee. It was decided to load it on Jack's jeep and try and flog it in Vienna. Although there were great shortages of practically everything at the time, they didn't sell any of it. It was just as well that none of them pursued a career in commerce.

It was an exciting and memorable posting. The Dakota was flown with VIPs as passengers. On one particular flight (29 July 46) they flew the Austrian Chancellor, Dr. Figl from Vienna to Graz. Mac was to meet him again, later, with my mother at a large cocktail party in Vienna. Dr. Leopold Figl, as Director of the Lower Austrian Farmer's League had spoken vociferously against the Nazi regime and was soon arrested when Hitler's Army entered Austria in March, 1938. He was sent to Dachau concentration camp where he was flogged and he was to spend over five years in Dachau, Flossenberg and Mauthausen. At the latter concentration camp he was charged with high treason and taken to Vienna, in March, 1945 for trial and execution. His incarceration ended when the Russian Army entered Vienna on 12th April. From April until December, 1945, Dr. Figl was the provincial Governor of Lower Austria but after elections in November, 1945, Karl Renner became President of Austria and Dr. Figl became Federal Chancellor of the Austrian government, a post he held until April, 1953. In 1953 he was replaced as Chancellor by his long standing friend Julius Raab, but in November he was appointed Foreign Minister and in this appointment Dr. Figl negotiated the State Treaty of 15th May, 1955 by which Austria became independent once more and proclaimed her neutrality.

When not flying in the Dakota, Mac would join Jack and fly off in the Auster. One day they went to ski. There was no skiing, either side of the Irish border and so it was a novel experience for both of them which they repeated a number of times. To go skiing, flying to the slopes in your own Auster was, to say the least, rather upmarket.

On 14 September 1946 my father got married to Marjorie Worrell, in Northwich, Cheshire, and after two weeks leave returned with my mother to Vienna. The General Officer Commanding (and High Commissioner) now General Steele, decided that the mess was unsuitable for them, so my mother and father moved to the Sachers Hotel, one of Vienna's finest. Each of the four occupying powers was giving an hotel where guests could be accomodated. The Americans were allocated the Bristol, the Russians took the Grand and the French the Hotel Kummer. The Sacher was situated opposite the Viennese State Opera, in the heart of the city, and was Vienna's first hotel to have electrified chandeliers. They stayed in five star accommodation, on full board and it cost them 2 shillings (10p) per person per day. At times the accommodation was very cold but my parents obtained, on occasions, coal from the Americans, to place in the exquisite fireplaces. In the post war situation, it was great luxury and an amazing experience so different from the simple way they both lived at home. After two months here, they moved into the three star Park Hotel, paid for by the army. After a short while there, they moved to the 'mess' which was now vacant.

As part of a very small community their social life revolved around the requirements of my father's job. They went to many cocktail parties and receptions, with all the 'top brass'; diplomats, journalists, politicians, and so on. On each of these occasions my father was able to request transport (with driver) from the General's car pool. On one such occasion after receiving an invitation to a ball, my father immediately ordered a car from the pool. They arrived at the ball in an open topped Mercedes Landau, reputedly a car used by Himmler. The General's ADC had reserved a car after Mac had done so. As my father and mother arrived at the ball in the Landau, the General, his wife and ADC were getting out of a basic Hillman. The General wasn't particularly pleased to see my parents in the Mercedes! General Steele also had a car pool in London. On one occasion my father arrived late in the evening in London (from Vienna) and requested transport to RAF Bassingbourne. The car allocated to him, with driver, was Churchill's old Rolls Royce. He had never travelled in such style since and the guard at the gate was quite shocked to see him arrive at RAF Bassingbourne. A mere Flight Lieutenant. Yes, it would not be hard to get used to this way of travelling.

Apart from military VIPs and politicians, (see Appendix 14) on the 1st October the crew flew six dancers from Sadlers Wells Ballet from London to Vienna. In a still drab post war Vienna, Sadlers Wells Ballet received many enthusiastic press notices. The 'WELT AM MONTAG' wrote "The London Sadlers Wells Ballet is the personified rejuvenation of the old ballet style, the perfection of classical technique……". The 'NEUES OSTERREICH' wrote "Now the Sadlers Wells Ballet has come to Vienna with its exquisite programme – Meyerbeer, Caesar, Franck, Gavin Gordon – and it appears as though doors and windows are flung open so that an air of really true dancing wafts towards us…….". After the Ballet one evening, Sqn Ldr Wainwright and my father were asked to escort Pamela May and Margot Fonteyn, respectively, to a reception. By all accounts it was a very enjoyable evening. Both the ladies were charming and very entertaining company.

A final tale of their life in the 'fast social lane' was at a reception for the Austrian Chancellor. After another enjoyable evening my mother and father found themselves in line, with the senior officers, waiting to bid goodbye, and shake hands with the Chancellor, Dr. Figl, as he and his guests were leaving. My mother, aged 24, being a nurse had assumed that he was a medical doctor and asked him which hospital he worked in. He replied "Madam, I am the Austrian Chancellor".

In February 1947, Mac was posted back with Sqn Ldr Wainwright and F/Lt Parkin, the navigator, to 24 Squadron, RAF Bassingbourne. They were still GOC air crew (General Officer Commanding) - General Steele, but not for much longer. On take off from Belfast (on 15th March) the port undercarriage hit a snow drift, driving it through the wing of the Dakota. They crash landed on Stretton airfield (South of Warrington, Cheshire). My father's sixth air crash. Fortunately, no one was hurt, but General Steele was rather unnerved by this. The whole crew were sacked from his staff, but they stayed with the VIP Squadron.

The crew continued flying to Vienna and other cities taking VIPs to their conferences and other events. They spent a fair bit of time flying in the Middle East. A VIP father remembers well was General Montgomery. He didn't drink or smoke unlike most aircrew in those days. Before any flight, he would shake hands with all the crew and put his head as near as he could to the crew members face, to see if he could detect any evidence of drinking. The crew members found this difficult as on one occasion they had been guests of the French Air Force in Paris, for 3 days. The French Air Force know how to entertain. Another habit of Montgomery's was to have his photograph taken, with the crew, after each flight. From Paris, they landed at RAF Northolt, to be greeted by the Station Group Captain. The Group Captain tried to get himself in the photograph. General Montgomery told him to "push off". The lower ranking aircrew loved that.

OCT 1946

Date	Hour	Aircraft Type and No.	Pilot	Duty	REMARKS (including results of bombing, gunnery, exercises, etc.)	Flying Times Day	Night
					Time carried forward :—	1720.50	276.00
1.10.46	KG528	DAKOTA	S/LDR WAINWRIGHT	WIRELESS OPERATOR	LONDON - VIENNA 6 Passengers from Sadlers Wells Ballet	5.20	
4.10.46	TS406	AUSTER	CAPTAIN FORSTER	CREW	VIENNA - SCHWECHAT	0.15	
4.10.46	KG528	DAKOTA	S/LDR WAINWRIGHT	WIRELESS OPERATOR	SCHWECHAT LOCAL 4 PASSENGERS.	0.30	
9.10.46	Do	Do	Do	-Do-	VIENNA - BERLIN CANCELLED AEROPLANE 4/5	0.35	
17.10.46	Do	Do	Do	Do	VIENNA LOCAL 1 PASSENGER	0.45	
20.10.46	Do	Do	Do	Do	VIENNA TO LONDON VIP MR MACK + 5 PASSENGERS	5.30	
29.10.46	Do	Do	Do	Do	NORTHOLT LOCAL 4 PASSENGERS	0.15/45	
30.10.46	Do	Do	Do	Do	NORTHOLT TO VIENNA VIA MR MACK + 4 PASSENGERS FIELD MARSHAL DEVERSON AND WIFE	6.10	
					TOTAL FOR MONTH	HRS 20	MNS 05
					TOTAL FLYING HOURS	HRS 1740	MNS 55
					SIGNED Michael Wainwright S/LDR		
					O/C AUSTRIAN COM FLT VIENNA.		
					TOTAL TIME ...		

Mac's Flying Log, October 1946 - Note Sadlers Wells Ballet Co. flight on 1st October

CHAPTER 9

IAN MACKENZIE

Ian Cumming MacKenzie was born in Brisbane, Australia on 13th July, 1922.

His father John Charles MacKenzie was born in 1892 in Longside, Aberdeenshire and served during World War 1 as a captain in the Gordon Highlanders. After the War, he immediately emigrated to Australia. He went to Queensland to meet up with his childhood sweetheart, Alice Mary Gill. She arrived in Brisbane, on the "SS Limerick" on 13th August 1913. She had previously been a teacher and lived in Old Deer, Mintlaw, and Rora in Aberdeenshire. They were married on 31st December, 1919 at Dakabin Farm (Gin Gin) Queensland and settled in Brisbane.

 From the day the war started, Ian wanted to be a pilot, preferably a fighter pilot. He even went to night school to learn about flying before he was old enough to join the forces. On the 20th August, 1940, at the height of the Battle of Britain, he joined the Royal Australian Air Force Reserves, while working as a storeman/packer for WD & HO Wills (Australia) Ltd, the tobacco company.

Ian enlisted for the RAAF proper on 5th January, 1941 at the No. 3 Recruiting Office in Brisbane. He was AC2 (Aircraftman 2) and went to No. 3 ITS (Initial Training School) at Sandgate. He became, after training an LAC (Leading Aircraftman) on the 1st March and was accepted for flying training which commenced 6 days later at No. 3 EFTS (Empire Flying Training School) at Tamworth, New South Wales. After 6 days flying instruction, Ian went solo in a Tiger Moth. Training continued on Oxford Airspeed and Anson aircraft, and as an LAC he received his "wings" in late June, 1941. On the 28th August he was promoted to Sergeant and on the 14th October, received his posting to the UK. He left Australia by boat the next day arriving in Southampton on 21st December. He never returned to Australia.

His first training flight in England was on 17th February, 1942 in an Oxford Airspeed, based at 14 (P) AFU at Ossington, near Newark. Two days later he went solo.

At 14 OTU Cottesmore in Rutland, Ian received more training, on Ansons and Hampdens. While there he met my father and future members of his crew. Initially the four man crew of Ian's Hampden comprised himself as pilot, Tiny Playfair as navigator, and my father and Con O'Connell as wireless operators/air gunners.

Ian's first operational trip was a baptism of fire. It was the third 1000 Bomber Raid, on Bremen on 25th June. Apart from this mission and one other, my father flew with Ian on all the other eighteen operations of Ian's.

His second trip was 'nickelling' Rennes, France. His comments after this operation were "easy trip – no trouble". His 4th trip, bombing Le Havre on the 11th August 1942 was described as "bang on". His 9th operation and last one flying a Hampden took place on the 7th September, to Frankfurt. He was now with 408 Squadron, RCAF based at RAF Balderton. This Squadron had the dubious honour of flying the last bombing operation in Hampden aircraft on 14th September. 408 Squadron was posted to RAF Leeming, Yorkshire to begin conversion training on the four engined Halifax bomber. It was during this time that Lloyd Mackenzie, RCAF joined the crew as Flight Engineer, Tommy Coupland, RAF as Bomb Aimer, and Rod Ball, RCAF as Air Gunner. Ian completed his training as a Halifax pilot and his summary (report) of Flying and Assessments stated that he was above average. "No outstanding faults. A sound confident pilot". Training continued throughout November and December and on 6th December Ian was commissioned as a Pilot Officer. It was time for the crew to get to know each other better and work as a team. To get to grips with new equipment and acquire the skills of flying in formation. The crew's first Halifax mission took place on the 15th January, 1943 bombing the U-Boat pens at Lorient.

The tragedy of the 15th April 1943 has previously been described. There is, however, more to tell. Ian's brother, Roy and cousin Ian, allowed me access to family correspondence. You will recall that before going on an operation, aircrew would leave 'a last letter home', as they collected their escape kit. Some of these letters were 'wills'. In the gung ho spirit of many aircrew, of which Ian was certainly a fine example, some 'letters' were written on scraps of paper or postcards. In Ian's case it was a postcard, written with one of his (few) prized possessions – a Conway Stewart fountain pen. His postcard is shown:

In event of my death or failure
to return from operations or I
be missing in any way all
my private gear & belongings
is to be sent to address
on other side [illegible] R.A.F. Esx

To Post address:
do this address

Miss C. Gill
401 Chiswick High Rd.
Gunnersbury.
London. W 4

(3501)

A.C.F.

His message was simple and to the point. It was almost as though Ian never expected the worst and to him, the writing of it was another formality. The date suggests he wrote it after his first 'op'. Miss Christine Gill was either a cousin or sister of his mother.

Records of all next-of-kin were held for aircrew. Apart from his father in Brisbane, Ian also named an aunt, Mrs. EE MacDonald who lived in Rora, Aberdeenshire. It was with his aunt and her family that Ian spent his last leave in March, 1943.

JB 909 was due back at RAF Leeming, from the Stuttgart operation at 5.47 am, 15th April, 1943. The following telegram was sent from RAF Leeming to Kingsway, London:

114

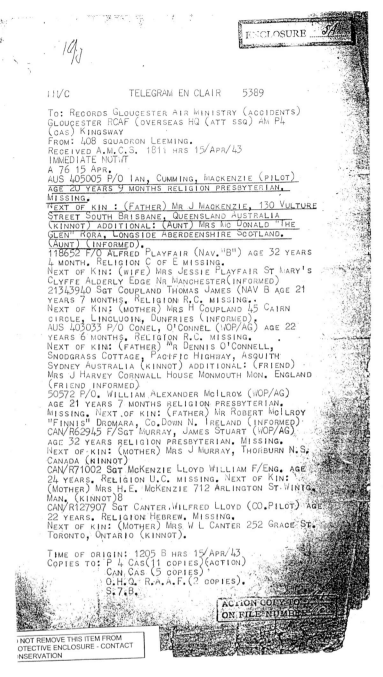

Immediately, a cipher telegram was sent to RAAF Headquarters in Melbourne and a similar telegram to RCAF Headquarters in Canada. Letters similar to those sent to my grandfather by the Squadron Commanding Officer and Padre would have been received by next-of-kin of each crew member. In Tiny Playfair's case, it was his wife. For the others it was to parents.

In Ian's case, the very sad fact is that he did not survive. His father was informed by the following letter, dated 19th May, 1943 from the Casuality Section, RAAF, South Yarra. It is not known whether Ian's father already knew the tragic news from other sources.

Dear Sir,

I deeply regret that I have to confirm the telegram from this Department dated 14th May, 1943 informing you that your son, Pilot Officer Ian Cumming MacKenzie previously reported missing is now reported missing but believed to have lost his life on the 15th April, 1943.

The change of classification has been made by the Air Ministry, London, in consequence of a report received from the International Red Cross Committee at Geneva, which states that according to

German information, your son lost his life as the result of air operations following which he was reported to be missing. I regret to state that the report does not give the place of your son's burial.

Permit me to again convey to you the sincere sympathy of this Department in your present anxiety, and I trust that the further leaflet enclosed will be of assistance to you.

Yours faithfully,

M.C.Langslow

Secretary

The tragedy of Ian's death is compounded by events after his death. Ian was the youngest crew member of JB 909 and the only one killed in action; three months before his 21st birthday. The following letter from his aunt, Mrs. E.E. MacDonald to Australia House, London, on 12th July, the day before Ian's birthday, indicates some optimism that he may have become a POW even though Ian's father knew otherwise.

Dear Sir,

I am rather at a loss to know where to write to about this small matter. Hope you do not find it too trivial.

My nephew, P/O Ian C MacKenzie, RAAF (from Brisbane) has been missing since the Stuttgart raid on April 14/15.

I have just had a letter from his father (Brisbane) saying that they had sent off his 21st birthday cake (for July13th, 1943) and am wondering if I can intercept it at this end and have it sent on to me here, so I can keep it for him, should he be reported a prisoner of war. It would be in a sealed tin.

What happens to those parcels arriving for boys who are missing? His parents managed to intercept his other 21st birthday gifts before the mail left Australia.

I shall be glad and grateful if you can help me. I am also writing to his squadron to see if it has arrived there – Leeming, Yorks.

Sincerely,

Mrs.E.E.Macdonald

A reply was sent to Mrs. MacDonald on 15th July.

Dear Mrs Macdonald,

Pilot Officer I.C.MacKenzie, Aus/405005

It is desired to acknowledge receipt of your letter fated 12th July, 1943 with reference to a birthday cake forwarded by Pilot Officer MacKenzie's people.

2. In reply to your enquiry as to what happens to such parcels addressed to personnel who are reported 'missing' it is desired to inform you that they are held at this Headquarters until three months from the date on which the member was reported 'missing', and unless instructions to the contrary have in the meantime been received from the senders through the Australian Air Board they are then opened to ascertain whether they contain any items of intrinsic or sentimental value in order that such items may be returned to the senders. The balance of the contents of these parcels are then passed to the Australian Red Cross Society for distribution amongst sick and wounded members of the Australian Forces in this Country.

3. This action is taken in regard to articles of food, even if a member is, in the meantime, reported as a Prisoner of War, as it is not possible to send individually addressed food parcels to prisoners of War

4. For reasons which it is considered you will appreciate this Headquarters is unable to forward parcels addressed to RAAF members who have been reported casualties to people in this Country without the authority of the sender, and in any case such parcels are admitted free of duty under special Customs Regulations on the distinct understanding that they be forwarded to members of the Fighting Services only.

5. Unless, therefore, you consider that Pilot Officers MacKenzie's parents particularly desire other action to be taken in regard to the disposal of the cake forwarded to him it is suggested that the normal procedure be followed, and that it be sent to the Australian Red Cross Society.

6. It is suggested that, for the reasons set out above, this Headquarters is unable to forward the parcel to you, but it is felt that you will agree that the proposed method of disposal is the most satisfactory under the circumstances.

Yours faithfully,

H.D.Winterbottom

Flight Lieutenant, for Air Vice Marshall

The reader may consider that the reply is rather matter of fact to the point where it is the product of an uncaring bureaucracy. The fact is that records had to be established and maintained and correct procedures had to be followed.

All property of missing aircrew was forwarded to RAF Colnbrook. From here all Ian's belongings were sent to Miss C Gill, in accordance with Ian's wishes. His bicycle, at RAF Leeming was sold, on the instructions of his mother, and proceeds added to any money he had left. Mrs. McKenzie asked Miss Gill to arrange with the RAAF in Kingsway to sell his uniforms and caps. The items raised £21-15-6d. (£21.77)

Further distress was inflicted on Ian's family in Australia and Scotland as they did not know where Ian was buried. The earliest confirmation may have come from a (POW) letter sent by Con O'Connell from Stalag Luft 111 to Miss Gill on 11th August.

Kriegsgefangenen post.

Miss.C.Gibbs

Empfangsort Chiswick Rd

Strabe CHISWICK

Kreis London

Land England

Absender

Vor Und Zuname P/O C.O'Connell

Gefangenennummer 1451

Lager Bezeichnung M Stammlager Luft 3

DEUTSCHLAND.

11.8.43.

Dear Chris, I have been meaning to drop you a line for some time past but was only able to get down to it today. I suppose you would have known we were missing for some time now. We were coming back from Stuttgart on the fourteenth of April and had reached France. Without any warning a flak battery opened up and before we could do anything we were hit pretty badly and started to burn. There was nothing we could do and as some of us were hit we decided to bale out. Mac was quite alright then and as I was the last out before he went I cannot understand how he did not escape. Unfortunately he was killed. The rest of us are alive although onis still in hospital. It was a terrible shock to all of us. When you write to Mac's mother would you tell her he was given a full military funeral and is buried in grave 10 Rheims cemetery France. Could you also send me her address. Mac and I were such good cobbers that it was like losing a brother. Give my regards to Ann & Tick and all the best

Yours sincerely

Con O'Connell

Ian was buried in grave 10 in the cemetery at La Neuvillette. The Germans gave him full military honours. The villagers covered his grave with flowers but the Germans removed them and placed a guard at the cemetery gate. Despite this, on the following nights some villagers still managed to go over the fence and place new flowers on the grave.

The first 'official' letter confirming the whereabouts of Ian's grave was received by RAAF Headquarters, London, from the International Red Cross Committee, Geneva. It was dated the 4th July, 1944.

After the war, P/O Ian MacKenzie's body was removed from La Neuvillette to an official war cemetery at Clichy, Paris. His grave can be found in Plot 16, Row 13, Grave 2. According to newspaper reports the citizens of La Neuvillette were not happy about this and decided to build their own memorial to Ian. In 1948 the then Mayor of Reims asked Australians to help with funds to build this memorial. The Sunday Mail (an Australian paper) set up a memorial fund.

A letter received by me from Ian MacKenzie's cousin, also called Ian MacKenzie, stated that the RAF, at the request of the RAAF, (at the request of the Prime Ministers Office) was trying to pinpoint why Ian stayed in the Halifax Bomber, JB 909. Cousin Ian MacKenzie speculated that the Australian Government was possibly embarrassed to find that a French town was going to erect a memorial and, and in addition, name a street after Ian whereas the Australian Government had failed to even decorate him.

My father submitted a letter to Bomber Command in July 1949. The following report appears on the RAAF Casualty file:

After carrying out a raid on Stuttgart, Halifax JB.909 was attacked and set on fire by an enemy fighter near Rheims. As the result of this attack Pilot Officer (now Flight Lieutenant) W.A. McIlroy, who was the tail gunner and is the only member of the crew still serving in the Royal Air Force, was wounded and completely cut off from communication with the rest of the crew. He consequently baled out independently. In reply to the letter sent from this Headquarters, Flight Lieutenant McIlroy states that he subsequently discussed this matter with the other members of the crew and was told that Pilot Officer MacKenzie was very worried because he (McIlroy) did not answer the order to bale out. From this evidence and that contained in the interrogation reports, it seems probable therefore that Pilot Officer MacKenzie, having inserted the automatic pilot, was making his way aft to see what had happened to McIlroy when the aircraft stalled and broke up and dived into the ground, where it exploded.

[MacKenzie, I.C.-RAAF Casualty File (NAA Series A705/15 Item 166/26/87)]

From this report came late recognition of Ian's bravery by the Australian government in the form of a Mention in Despatches (MID). Ian's MID as follows:

Summary of Services

Mention-in-Despatches

(posthumous)

Pilot Officer I.C. MacKenzie (Aus.405005), Royal Australian Air Force, No.408 (R.C.A.F) Squadron

Pilot Officer MacKenzie was the pilot of a Halifax aircraft which was attacked by enemy fighters near Rheims when returning from a bomber raid on Stuttgart one night in April, 1943. The aircraft was set on fire and became extremely difficult to control. When it was found that the fire could not be extinguished the pilot gave the order to abandon aircraft. The last member of the crew to leave the burning aircraft was the flight engineer who has reported that there was no apparent reason why the Pilot should not have followed suit. As a result of investigation it now transpires that the Pilot was "very worried" at receiving no acknowledgement of his order from the tail-gunner being unaware that he had previously been wounded and had baled out independently. Pilot Officer MacKenzie was seen to set his automatic pilot with the intention of making his way to the tail-gunner's position. This no doubt caused the badly damaged aircraft to stall and dive to the ground. Pilot Officer MacKenzie could have saved himself but his concern for the safety of the crew (all of whom escaped) and his determination to make sure that all had left the aircraft caused him to sacrifice his life. His action was in every way in accordance with the highest traditions of the Air Force.

Official recognition at last, to a very brave young pilot who was only twenty years old. As referred to earlier, the French authorities made no award, which remains a puzzle to the MacKenzie family.

As referred to earlier, Ian was buried in the cemetery at La Neuvillette with full German military honours.

Ian's memorial was officially unveiled on 15th April, 1955, twelve years after he was killed. The Australian Ambassador to France (Alfred Stirling) laid a wreath as did other dignatories from several countries and organisations. Pierre Closterman, the French air ace, also attended the ceremony, one of two thousand to do so.

After the plane exploded on impact, a Madame Lefevre removed a propeller blade from the crash site in a pram. She kept it in her attic for 40 years. In 1983, when Ian MacKenzie (cousin) attended the 40th anniversary of the crash, she presented the blade to him. He, in turn, offered it to Wg Cdr Cairns, the then RAAF Air Attaché in Paris. It is now located in the RAAF Museum at Point Cook in Australia. Madame Lefevre's mother, pictured, was a member of the Comete Line escape committee of the French Resistance. She was captured by the Germans and died in Ravensbruck concentration camp, north of Berlin. Her work and sacrifice was recognised by the US, UK and French Governments and accordingly posthumously decorated by all three.

Another part of the plane, bearing the serial number, was also removed from the site. It was later given to Mrs MacKenzie, the pilot's mother in 1972 when she visited La Neuvillette, after a six week journey to France by boat from Australia. She gave it to her other son, Roy MacKenzie, who presented it to the Commander of 408 Sqn. It is now in a dedicated corner for 408 Sqn in the RCAF Museum in Edmonton, Canada.

What is very extraordinary is that my father was unaware of Ian's memorial in La Neuvillette until February, 2005. If only he had known, my father would have gone to Reims in 1972 to meet Ian MacKenzie's mother, when she visited her son's memorial. My father was still in the RAF at this time.

CHAPTER 10

LA NEUVILLETTE AND REIMS

A very good friend of mine, Mike Garland, discovered the memorial on a website, which prompted me to write to the Town Hall in Reims for information and details. The Town Hall staff kindly responded with an invitation to the 60th anniversary celebrations to mark the end of the war, on 7th May, 2005. I travelled to Reims to the celebrations and whilst there visited Ian's memorial. On my return to England I told my father about my visit and he understandably expressed a wish to see it. Later that same month, I returned to Reims, with Mac.

Before this visit I again wrote to the Town Hall. On our arrival at the Kyriad Centre Hotel in Reims, we were presented with a dossier, from Mr Roger Vache, Deputy Mayor of Reims. He and his colleagues Mr. Stephane Damian and Mme Dominique Ingret-Dunaime had arranged a number of visits and functions for my father and me. To say we were amazed at this extraordinary hospitality and courtesy would be an understatement. After a champagne reception in the stunning Hotel de Ville, where we met journalists, historians, writers and veterans, we were chauffeur driven in the Mayor's limousine to the Surrender Museum for a private tour of the museum by its director, Mark Bouxin. My father was photographed sitting at the table where the surrender document was signed by the German General, Alfred Jodl on 7th May, 1945. After this, we were taken to the memorial for Ian in La Neuvillette, in the now named Rue Jean MacKenzie. It was a very moving moment for my father, as he cast his mind back 62 years to the events which he had tried to block out over the subsequent years. There was a two minute silence by the memorial, as a French flag was slowly lowered by a French veteran, in front of the memorial. It was a poignant moment. I felt particularly proud, and very humbled. I cast my own mind back to when I was 20 years old. I had done nothing to compare with the deeds of those airmen, soldiers and sailors, fighting for their countries. They were risking and losing their lives. Very different world, a very different generation.

After this moving ceremony, the party returned to Reims for lunch. My father had brought his 'scrap book' and flying records for the assembled company to view. It was during lunch that he mentioned the Red Cross Nurse, Mme Chatelin who had so kindly visited him, (and Alex

Ager) with her young daughter. While we were still at the table, Town Hall staff managed to trace the daughter, Mm Francoise Hebert, who lived in Reims with her husband Claude. It was her son, Eric, who gave me the information about Sergeant Canters likely escape journey to freedom after the Halifax Bomber was shot down. Mme Chatelin, as noted previously, was arrested by the Gestapo. To maintain the integrity and preserve the neutrality of the Red Cross Mme Chatelin had to be seen to have no connection with the activities of the French Resistance and Escape Lines. The Germans did not know about her work. The day she was arrested, Mme Chatelin's daughter, Francoise, was in the house. Francoise was told to "go into the cellar and tidy". She went down to the cellar because she felt something was wrong. She found RAF uniforms. She hid them quickly then cycled to a cousin's farm, 10 miles away.

My father was amazed and delighted that Francoise had been located. After the sumptuous lunch, we visited Maison Blanche (American Memorial Hospital) We were unable to see the room my father occupied at this time, although he had seen it on a visit to Reims in 1965. On that visit he saw the bar on the window where the Canadian Officer attempted to cut through with a hacksaw blade with the intention of escaping. The return visit, this time, brought back good and bad memories. A German surgeon saved his right leg and possibly his life. The painful memories included being locked up, constantly hungry, often lonely, and worst of all the unremitting torment of bed bugs and fleas in the plastercast.

At the end of our first day we were whisked to Mr & Mrs Hebert's apartment to meet them and their son Eric. What a wonderful occasion, a reunion! Mm Hebert was about 15 years old when she visited, with her mother, Mme Chatelin, in 1943. My father when he himself was 21. Mme Hebert was a very competent English speaker and she and my father had much to talk about. So much so that we hardly noticed the newspaper photographer arriving to take pictures. We spent the next two evenings with the wonderfully hospitable Hebert family.

The following day we were taken, by Eric, a fluent English speaker, and an aviation historian, Jacques Pernet, to BA 112, a large French air base near Reims. Here there is a museum in which one exhibit is dedicated solely to Ian MacKenzie and his Halifax Bomber. It is a wonderful museum depicting the history of flight. A copy of my father's flying log, showing the date he was shot down is now a part of the exhibit, with a picture of the crew (as shown). The Commander of the base came to meet us before we left.

On our return to Reims from the air base, Eric stopped to purchase the L'Union newspaper, one of the main papers covering Northern France. To our surprise, there was a picture on the front page, of my father, Mm Hebert and myself. Inside the paper (Page 10) was an article about my father's 'pilgrimage' to Reims, with two photographs, one of the crew of the Halifax and one of him signing the visitor's book at the Surrender Museum. The excellent newspaper article was written by Herve Chabaud, whose own relatives suffered at the hands of the Nazis.

The Town Hall not only arranged another superb lunch but also made arrangements for a private visit to the Verve Cliquot Champagne Cellars. It was a very interesting visit, ending with a very special 1985 pink champagne.

We left Reims with poignant memories. Memories of events of the past few days and of the many years before. We also left with a strong affection for the many French people we had met, who had been so generous to us. In response to our desire to reciprocate, there was a common message. My father and his comrades in the war had helped liberate France. They said that was more than sufficient.

My father and I intend to return to Reims. The French people remember those days. We must remember them too.

POST-SCRIPT

Our visit to Reims generated considerable interest and stimulated me to write this book. I have heard on many occasions that the generation who fought in the war were reluctant to speak about their experiences. I have spoken to a number of relatives during the course of research and many have regretted not speaking to, or asking, their fathers (and mothers) what they did in the war. Those experiences and anecdotes are lost forever. This urged me on to record and describe my father's experiences as best I could. Having no experience whatsoever of what my father, and thousands of others went through, it is appropriate, I think, to expose some of their collective modesty. They were all heroes. In the course of writing this account, I traced the whereabouts of Alex Ager, Mac's fellow 'Kriegie' in Reims Hospital in 1943. There was a wonderful re-union between these two gentlemen in January, 2006. I have been in regular contact with Bill Lott, the bomb aimer whose poetry captured the moment.

There is an extraordinary irony to this story. You may recall that the Halifax Bomber was returning to England after having successfully bombed Stuttgart. Cousin Ian MacKenzie, residing in Scotland has two daughters. One of these daughters is married to a German. In Germany, children may take the surname of their mothers. And so the only male MacKenzie, in this family, is half German, and lives in Stuttgart.

APPENDICES

1. Units Served

2. List of Operations 1942-1943

3. French Police Report, April 1943

4. Communications with POWs

5. Particulars of Service Clothing

6. Canter Escape Report

7. London Restaurant Recommendations

8. Hotel Recommendations

9. Wine Recommendations

10. Selection of Menus and Recipes

11. Red Cross Parcel Contents

12. Books Read

13. Plays and Shows

14. VIPs Flown

APPENDIX 1

UNITS SERVED

Jan 1939	- March 1939	RAF Cardington
March 1939	- 3 Sep 1939	RAF Yatesbury
7 Oct 1939	- 21 Oct 1940	RAF St Athan School of Air Navigation
21 Oct 1940	- 23 Apr 1942	RAF Cranage, with attachment to RAF North Weald
23 Apr 1942	- 9 July 1942	No14 OTU RAF Cottesmore
9 Jul 1942	- 19 Sep 1942	408 Sqn, RCAF Balderton
19 Sep 1942	- 15 Apr 1943	408 Sqn, RCAF Leeming

---

15 Apr 1943	- 4 Jan 1944	Reims Hospital
4 Jan 1944	- 18 Jan 1944	Journey to Stalag Luft III
18 Jan 1944	- 27 Jan 1945	Stalag Luft III, Sagan
27 Jan 1945	- 3 Feb 1945	March to Stalag III A
3 Feb 1945	- 4 May 1945	At Luckenwalde
4 May 1945	- 7 May 1945	Escape to American 9th Army, on the Elbe
11 May 1945		Hanover to Reims
12 May 1945		Repatriated to Oxford

Nov 1945	- Feb 1946	1383 TCU RAF Crosby on Eden
Feb 1946	-	24 Sqn RAF Hendon Transport
March 1946		24 Sqn RAF Bassingbourne
April 1946		Austrian Communication Sqn, Vienna
Feb 1947		24 Sqn RAF Bassingbourne

APPENDIX 2

OPERATIONS

1942	30 May	Cologne	1000 Bomber Raid
	1 June	Essen	ditto
	25 June	Bremen	ditto
	19 July	N W Germany	
	26 July	Hamburg	
	3 Aug	Kiel	
	5 Aug	Rennes	
	9 Aug	Freisan Islands	
	11 Aug	Le Havre	
	15 Aug	Düsseldorf	
	27 Aug	Kassel	
	28 Aug	Saarbrucken	
	6 Sept	Duisburg	
	7 Sept	Frankfurt	
1943	15 Jan	Lorient	
	3 Feb	Hamburg	
	7 Feb	Lorient (from MacKenzie log)	
	15 Feb	Cologne	
	24 Feb	Wilhelmshaven	
	26 Feb	Cologne	
	8 March	Nuremburg	
	12 March	Essen	
	22 March	St Nazaire	
	26 March	Duisburg	
	27 March	Berlin	
	3 April	Essen	

8 April	Duisburg
14 April	Stuttgart

N.B.   My fathers log book recorded 27 operations, but, in fact he flew 28. A trip to Lorient on 7 February 1943 was not recorded. This information was obtained from Pilot Ian MacKenzie's flying log.

All operations in 1942, in Hampdens.

All operations in 1943, in Halifaxes.

APPENDIX 3

FRENCH POLICE REPORT

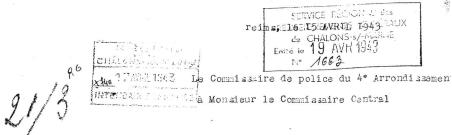

reims, le 15 AVRIL 1943

Le Commissaire de police du 4° Arrondissement
à Monsieur le Commissaire Central

Objet - Chute d'un avion anglais à La Neuvillette

J'ai l'honneur de vous rendre compte de la chute d'un
avion anglais abattu cette nuit par un chasseur allemand au-
dessus de la péréphirie de Reims, chute au sujet de laquelle j'ai
où obtenir à l'heure actuelle, les renseignements suivants :
A deux heures 55, un avion anglais ppis en charge par un
appareil allemand a été touché par une rafale de mitrailleuse et
a pris feu. Après avoir tenu l'air pendant 7 à 8 minutes, il s'est
abattu sur le territoire de la Neuvillette, à 1 kilomètre au delà
du pont du canal et environ 1 kilomètre sur la droite. La queue
de l'avion a été trouvée à 800 mètres après le pont du canal et
à 50 mètres en bordure, coté droit, de la route qui mène à Laon.
M. le Capitaine de gendarmerie Auzas s'est rendu sur les lieu
et a procédé aux constatations d'usage.
D'après les déclarations qui auraient été faites à cet of-
ficier, par l'un des occupants, blessé, l'équipage se composait de
huit hommes dont plusieurs ont pu sauter en parachute.
A l'heure où nous avons recueilli ces renseignements, il y
aurait un homme blessé à la cuisse, découvert à 2 ou 300 mètres
avant Cernay et transporté à l'hôpital de la maison Blanche;
1 dont on ignore le point de chute, conduit au même hôpital par
les Allemands, 3 pris vivants par les Allemands et transférés
à Courcy, 1 serait visible sous les débris de l'appareil; on ignor
ce qu'il est advenu des deux autres.
Le gardien de la Paix Bertrand, détaché à la Neuvillette qui
s'était immédiatement transporté sur les lieux a été prié de se
retirer par la gendarmerie allemande.
Il n'est pas à ma connaissance que des balles de mitrail-
leuses retombées en ville aient provoqué des accidents.
Le Commissaire de Police
signé :CHARBONNEAU

VU et TRANSMIS à :
M. le PREFET REGIONAL (S.P.)
M. LE PREFET de la MARNE(Cabinet)
M. le SOUS-PREFET,REIMS
M. le MAIRE de REIMS
REIMS, le 15 AVRIL 1943
Le Commissaire Central P. LUNDY :

APPENDIX 4

COMMUNICATION WITH POWs

IMPORTANT : FOR A PRISONER IN GERMAN HANDS THE PRISONER OF WAR No. MUST
BE CLEARLY SHOWN.   IT MUST NOT BE CONFUSED WITH HIS BRITISH
SERVICE No.

PRISONER OF WAR POST

KRIEGSGEFANGENENPOST
SERVICE DES PRISONNIERS DE GUERRE

RANK & NAME:...
(SURNAME IN BLOCK LETTERS)

British Prisoner of War

PRISONER OF WAR No.:...
(SEE NOTE ON FLAP)

CAMP NAME & No.:...
(INCLUDING SUBSIDIARY
NUMBERING OR LETTERING
IF ANY—E.G. WORKING CAMP)

COUNTRY:..

P 2280E
(Revd. 24376/41)

COMMUNICATION WITH PRISONERS OF WAR AND CIVILIANS INTERNED ABROAD.

1. This leaflet applies primarily to British (including Dominion and Colonial) prisoners of war interned in enemy and neutral countries ; but paragraphs 2-4 as regards the Letter Post are also applicable to letters and postcards addressed to prisoners of war of other nationalities interned abroad. The term " Prisoners of War " includes all interned persons, naval, military, air force and civilian.

British Service men who are in the hands of the French (Vichy) Government do not come into the same category as prisoners of war, and relatives should apply to the Foreign Relations Department, British Red Cross and St. John War Organisation, Warwick House, St. James's, London, S.W.1, for information regarding communications with these men.

LETTER POST.

2. Letters and postcards may be sent post free by ordinary post (for air-mail facilities *see* paragraph 5). They should be posted in the ordinary way and should not be sent to the British Red Cross Society to be forwarded. They should be clearly written or typed, and letters should not exceed two sides of a normal sized sheet of notepaper ; otherwise they are liable to delay and may even not be delivered by the authorities in the country to which they are addressed.

In the interests of the prisoners, relatives should limit their letters to one or two a week ; the more that are sent the more are they likely to be delayed by the censorship abroad. For the same reason letters from strangers are to be deprecated.

Letters and postcards must only deal with purely personal matters, and care should be taken that no information of any kind which might be of use to the enemy is given. No references to naval, military, aerial, economic or political matters are allowed, and movements of any members of His Majesty's Forces or any warship or merchant ship must not be mentioned.

3. **Enclosures.**—No enclosures are allowed in the air letter card (*see* paragraph 5).

Any enclosure in a letter may cause delay. Snapshots or unmounted photographs of a personal nature are, however, allowed and simple bank statements (not pass books) may be sent. International reply coupons must not be sent ; their use for the prepayment of air mail letters is unnecessary and is not permitted. Picture postcards, birthday or greetings cards bearing pictorial illustrations and pictorial matter of any kind are forbidden. The Letter Post may be used only for letters and postcards and must on no account be used for sending small articles such as packets of razor blades, chocolate, etc. ; such items may be sent only in the next of kin parcel (*see* paragraph 14).

4. **Method of Address.**—It is of the utmost importance that the details of the address should be correct and correspondents should make sure that they use the latest address supplied by the prisoner. In the case of prisoners in German hands the address is usually given on the back of

Specimen Address.

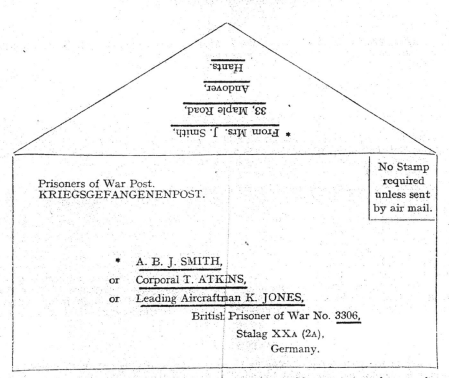

```
                                       Hants.
                                      Andover,
                                  33, Maple Road,
                              * From Mrs. J. Smith,
```

Prisoners of War Post. KRIEGSGEFANGENENPOST.	No Stamp required unless sent by air mail.

* A. B. J. SMITH,

or   Corporal T. ATKINS,

or   Leading Aircraftman K. JONES,

British Prisoner of War No. 3306,

Stalag XXA (2A),

Germany.

* The details underlined in the foregoing specimen addresses are merely examples and care should be taken that the appropriate details furnished in letters sent by the prisoner are inserted in the address of letters sent to him.

their letter cards or postcards, in particular the Camp number is shown after the words " Lager—Bezeichnung." The address should be clearly written in INK both on the envelope and on the letter itself. The use of adhesive address labels or previously used envelopes is strictly forbidden.

(i) **For prisoners whose prisoner of war number and camp address are known.**—No mention should be made either in the address or in the letter of the unit or regiment in which the prisoner of war was serving at the time of his capture. The following particulars should be given :—

(a) Rank (unless the addressee is an interned civilian), initials and surname (preferably in block letters).

(b) British Prisoner of War (or British Interned Civilian).

(c) Prisoner of War Number. (For prisoners in German hands this number is a most important element of the address. Care should be taken to quote it correctly ; it should not be confused with the service number given him by the British authorities. Prisoners in Italian hands are not given a prisoner of war number and the British Service number should be quoted.)

(d) Camp address. (It is important that the Camp address should be complete, e.g., in the specimen address on page 1 " Stalag " means " permanent camp " and is insufficient without the addition of the appropriate number, including any subsidiary lettering or numbers giving perhaps details of a working Camp subordinate to the parent Camp, e.g., Stalag XXA (2A)).

(e) Country.

The top left-hand corner of the envelope should bear the words " Prisoners of War post," and if addressed to a prisoner of war in German hands, the equivalent word " KRIEGSGEFANGENENPOST " should be added, or if addressed to a prisoner of war in Italian hands the words " Service des prisonniers de guerre." The name and address of the sender should be written on the back of the envelope. If, however, the sender is serving in His Majesty's Forces, whether at home or abroad, he must on no account give the address of his unit ; instead he should state the address of a relative or friend in this country who would be willing to send on any letters received from the prisoner.

(ii) **For prisoners in German hands whose prisoner of war number and/or camp address have not yet been announced.**

Letters may be addressed to such prisoners of war as follows :—

Regtl. No.............. Rank.............. Name....................
(Block letters).

British Prisoner of War,
P/W Number (if known),
C/o Agence Centrale des prisonniers de guerre,
Comité International de la Croix-Rouge,
Geneva,
Switzerland.

(iii) **For prisoners in Italian hands whose camp address has not yet been announced.**

Letters may be addressed to such prisoners of war as follows :—

Regtl. No.............. Rank.............. Name....................
(Block letters)

British Prisoner of War,
C/o Croce Rosse Italiana,
6 Via Puglie,
Rome.

It should, however, be particularly noted that as soon as the prisoner of war number and the camp address have been received for prisoners in German hands, and as soon as the camp address has been received for prisoners in Italian hands, letters should be addressed directly to the camp (as under 4 (1)). Failure to do so will cause delay.

5. **Air Mail.**—(a) An **air letter card** specially designed for writing to prisoners of war is on sale at most Post Offices. It costs 3d., and goes all the way to Germany or Italy by air. No enclosures may be sent.

(b) Letters and postcards may be prepaid at the rate of 5d. for the first ounce and 3d. for each additional ounce (postcards 2½d.). They should bear a blue air mail label in the top left hand corner. They go by air all the way to Germany or Italy.

(c) All letters and postcards **from** prisoners of war in Germany and Italy are brought by air from Lisbon to this country free of charge. Those from Germany travel by air from Germany to Lisbon free of charge. It is hoped shortly to arrange for similar facilities for letters from Italy.

N.B.—**No attempt should be made to communicate with Prisoners of War through people in neutral countries ; letters forwarded by prisoners through intermediaries in neutral countries do not receive the privilege of free air mail transmission from Lisbon.**

PARCEL POST.

Parcels for Prisoners of War in Enemy (or Enemy-occupied) Countries.

6. Parcels cannot be despatched by relatives direct to a prisoner of war. Food, clothing, soap and tobacco are sent regularly to prisoners in enemy countries by the British Red Cross Society and Order of St. John of Jerusalem (see paragraph 9), and " next-of-kin " parcels for prisoners in enemy countries may be sent under the arrangement explained in paragraph 12 of this leaflet. A card of acknowledgment for signature and return by the prisoner is enclosed in every parcel despatched. For parcels for prisoners of war in neutral countries see paragraphs 17-19.

7. In addition to the parcels sent by the Red Cross, orders may be given to firms holding special permits for the **direct** despatch of parcels containing books, music, packs of cards, games, tobacco and cigarettes (*see* paragraphs 20 and 22). Parcels may not be sent by air mail.

8. Customs Duty is not normally charged on parcels sent to prisoners ; and the Customs Declarations and Despatch Notes which usually have to be prepared by the senders of foreign parcels are not required.

NOTE.—Parcels or packets posted otherwise than in accordance with this leaflet will be returned to the sender.

Parcels sent by the British Red Cross.

9. **Food** and, except as set out in paragraph 22, **Tobacco** cannot be sent by relatives to a prisoner of war. Food, soap, cigarettes and tobacco at the cost of 10s. per parcel are sent to British, Dominion and Colonial prisoners of war in enemy territory by the British Red Cross and St. John War Organisation. Contributions towards defraying this expenditure will be gratefully accepted. Such contributions should be sent to the Accountant, Prisoners of War Department, St. James's Palace, London, S.W.1, or to the Scottish Red Cross, 206, Bath Street, Glasgow, C.2. These contributions will be paid into the funds of the Prisoners of War Department to defray the cost of the food parcels sent to all prisoners. (Postage must be paid on letters addressed to the Red Cross Society.)

10. **Invalid Comforts.**—The Invalid Comforts Section despatches consignments of ordinary household drugs together with such things as cod liver oil and malt, invalid food and comforts addressed to the Camp Leader of the Prisoners of War Camps, in order that in the case of illness or minor injuries, that are not sufficiently severe for hospital treatment, remedies may be at hand when needed.

Relatives may, in certain circumstances, send an invalid comforts parcel every twelve weeks, but they must first communicate with the Hon. Secretary, Invalid Comforts Section, 14, Carlton House Terrace, London, S.W.1, for authorisation, as each case is considered on its merits. At the request of the relatives or the Senior Officer of the Camp, individual food parcels can be arranged for serious or chronic cases requiring special diet, in place of the standard food parcels. Invalid Comforts food parcels are sent to all hospitals where it is known there are British Prisoners of War. Surgical appliances such as spectacles, dentures and other urgently needed requisites can be sent through the Invalid Comforts Section.

11. **Clothing.**—The British Government supplies all clothing for Prisoners of War (*i.e.*, greatcoats, battledress or uniform, boots, underclothing, towels, etc.). The British Red Cross Society arranges for its packing and despatch.

" Next of Kin " Parcels for Prisoners in Enemy (or Enemy-occupied) Countries.

12. Once every three months the next of kin of a prisoner in enemy territory is allowed to send him a " next of kin " parcel. The parcel must not weigh more than 10 lb. when packed, so that when repacked it comes within the international limit of weight. Each parcel must bear a special tie-on label which will be sent quarterly direct to the next of kin by the British Red Cross Society. The sender must fill in the label, which will then bear an address in the following form :—

Prisoner of War NEXT OF KIN PARCEL.

Regimental No............. Prisoner of War No. ....
Rank................. Name......................
Camp....................
C/o British Red Cross Society & Order of St. John,
14, Finsbury Circus,
London, E.C.2.

The address must also be copied in ink on the cover of the parcel. Unless the parcel bears the special label, it will not be accepted at a Post Office. No postage is required. If the sender requires an acknowledgment of the receipt of the parcel at Finsbury Circus, a stamped addressed postcard should be enclosed.

13. **Packing.**—The parcels should be packed as for the inland post. The name and address of the sender must be clearly written on the cover of the parcel, except that if the sender is serving in His Majesty's Forces he must not write his own address but must give the address of a relative or friend and may request the relative or friend to forward any acknowledgments received in respect of the parcel. A duplicate list of the contents must be put inside the parcel ; forms for this purpose are sent with the tie-on label by the British Red Cross Society.

14. **Permissible Articles.**—Among the articles which may be sent are the following :—
Attaché cases.
Blankets. Boots, boot laces ; gum boots. Brilliantine in tins. Brushes of all kinds.
Button-cleaning outfits (solid, not liquid polish).
Chewing gum. Solid chocolate in slabs (no filling).
Cigarette filter tips and cigarette rolling machine but NOT cigarettes or cigarette papers.
Clothing, including underwear, civilian or Service shirts, any footwear, knitted comforts or uniform. (See paragraph 15 for prohibited articles.)
Coloured silks and cottons, plain linen or canvas for embroidering.
Dentrifice (solid or powder but NOT in tubes).
Frames with talc or unbreakable glass.
Hussifs containing usual items.
Kit bags (without locks or metal eye holes). Knitting needles and wool.
Pencils. Pipes and tobacco pouch.
Safety razors and blades. Safety tin openers.
Shoe polish (solid, not liquid or in tubes). Shoe leather and nails for mending ; metal studs for toes and heels.
Small musical instruments.
Soap of all kinds. Towels, face cloths and sponges.

4

15. Prohibited Articles.—The following articles may not be enclosed :—
    (i) Written communications (letters must be sent separately).
    (ii) Printed matter.
    (iii) Pictorial illustrations and photographs.
    (iv) Money, stamps, stationery and playing cards.
    (v) Articles in tubes, tins and other receptacles which cannot easily be opened for inspection.
    (vi) Candles, spirits or solidified spirit for cooking stoves, matches or any other inflammable material.
    (vii) Photographic apparatus, field glasses, sextants, compasses, electric torches and other instruments of use for naval and military purposes.
    (viii) Haversacks.
    (ix) Complete suits, coloured or grey flannel trousers, corduroy trousers, black or coloured shirts normally worn without coats, sports coats or blazers, mackintoshes, or any kind of overcoat. (These items of clothing, however, may be sent to civilians.)
    (x) Food, tobacco, cigarettes. (*See* paragraphs 9 and 22.)
    (xi) Medical comforts. This includes medicines of all kinds, drugs and bandages.
    (xii) Watches ; Scissors (except small or nail scissors) ; knives and tools.
    (xiii) Pen nibs and fountain pens.

16. Return of Prohibited Articles.—On receipt in London of a next of kin parcel it will be repacked under the supervision of a representative of the Censorship, and any prohibited articles will be withdrawn and returned to the sender.

Parcels for Prisoners of War in Neutral Countries.

17. Address.—Parcels for prisoners of war in neutral countries must be forwarded through the British Red Cross Society. No special label is necessary and parcels should be addressed in the same way as letters (*see* paragraph 4) with the addition of the following :—

c/o British Red Cross Society,
14, Finsbury Circus,
London, E.C.2.

No postage is required.

18. Packing.—Parcels when packed must not weight more than 10 lb. each and should be packed as for the inland post. A list of the contents should be put inside.

19. Contents.—Neither the articles numbered (i) to (ix) in paragraph 15 nor food may be sent. In order that any prohibited article may be returned to the sender his name and address should be written on the cover, as described in paragraph 13.

Parcels and Packets sent by Permit Holders.

20. Books, Music, Packs of Cards, Games and Sports Equipment.—Many of the leading publishers and newsagents, etc., hold a special permit from the Censorship Department, which enables them to execute and despatch orders for books, music, packs of cards and games for prisoners of war in enemy or neutral countries. Holders of permits can accept only orders for despatch direct ; they can in no case accept books, etc., for forwarding to prisoners.

21. Newspapers and Periodicals.—These may be sent in the same way as books to prisoners of war in neutral countries, but not to prisoners of war in enemy territory.

22. Tobacco and Cigarettes.—These may be sent to prisoners of war and interned civilians in enemy and enemy-occupied countries and prisoners of war in neutral countries by firms who hold a special permit from the Censorship Department. Orders should be placed with these firms by relatives desiring to take advantage of the arrangement The minimum quantity which may be sent free of duty in one parcel is 4 oz. net.

23. Parcels (but not packets) despatched to neutral countries by permit holders must be accompanied by the appropriate number of Customs Declarations and Despatch Notes. The maximum limit of weight for parcels despatched to neutral or enemy countries is 11 lb.

Educational Books.

24. The Educational Books Section of the British Red Cross Society arranges for prisoners of war to continue their preparation for examinations, and enables them to undertake vocational training with a view to preparing themselves for the after-war period. The Society gives advice, and arranges for books to be sent to any prisoner wishing to read a special subject. Forms of request for these books are sent to the prison camps. Financial contributions from relatives and friends are invited, but when these cannot be given the Society undertakes the whole cost. Correspondence courses cannot be sent direct to prisoners of war, but on application to the Society help will be given as to possible means of despatch.

Telegrams.

25. Telegrams making inquiry regarding the welfare or whereabouts of prisoners of war cannot be sent to countries abroad. Such inquiries must be addressed to the British Red Cross Society, The Lord Chamberlain's Office, St. James's Palace, London, S.W.1.

There is no telegraph service to prisoners of war, but in cases of grave emergency only it is sometimes possible for the British Red Cross Society to send a message to the International Red Cross Committee in Geneva for them to pass on to their representative in Berlin or Rome to send to the prisoner concerned. Inquiries regarding the despatch of messages in such cases should be addressed to the British Red Cross Society at the address shown above.

General Post Office.

August, 1941.

[8/4] S.O. 688 Wt. 27922—2844 50m 9/42 H & S, Ltd. Gp. 404/12631 T.S. 10174

APPENDIX 5

PARTICULARS OF SERVICE CLOTHING

APPENDIX 'D'
(Annexure 'C')

POST HOSTILITIES EVACUATION OF PRISONERS
OF THE UNITED KINGDOM AND THE CONTINENT.

Particulars of Service Clothing issued to Officers during
Captivity.

1. For information of Officers.

Supplies of clothing from Army and R.A.F. stocks are sent to Geneva
through the agency of the British Red Cross Society, for distribution in the
Camps in which British Commonwealth prisoners are detained in Europe.

Since R.A.F. Officers are responsible for the maintenance of their
clothing, and will have received Income Tax Relief in respect of the upkeep of
their kit during the period of their captivity, they will be required to make
some payment for items of clothing received from public sources while in captivity
or en route of repatriation.

When items are handed in or left behind at the Prisoners of War Camp or
returned to store at the Reception Unit the charge will be assessed according to
the length of time the garments have been used, and where the garments are
retained the sum will depend upon their condition when received.

It is therefore necessary for each officer to complete this pro-forma
in order that the amount recoverable to the public can be assessed on as fair
and reasonable a basis as possible, and so that the settlement of accounts can
be expedited.

2.   To be completed by the Officer.

13.5.48.

I was repatriated to the United Kingdom on ....
During captivity or en route I received the following items of Service clothing,
which have either been left behind in the Prisoner of War Camp, returned or
retained by me, as indicated:-

	R.A.F. Number or recd. Army.	Left behind, returned or retained. Which.	Approximate time in use if left behind or returned.	Condition upon receipt (whether new or part worn) if retained.
War Service Dress - blouse.	—	—	—	—
Tunic or battle dress blouse.	—	—	—	—
*Trousers.	Army 1	Left Behind	15 mths	
*Greatcoat.	Army (American) 1	- do -	2 Yrs	
*Cap field Service.	Army (American) 1	Retained		Part worn
Pullover.	—	—	—	—
Boots. (pair)	Army (American) 1	Retained	—	New
*Shirt.	- Do - 1	- do -	— do —	
Collar.	—	—	—	—
Tie.	—	—	—	—

R.A.F. Number (contd.)

	R.A.F. Number or ARMY	Left behind or returned, retained. Thief.	Approximate time in use if left behind or returned.	Condition upon receipt whether new or part worn if retained.
Vest Woollen.	ARMY (AMERICAN) 1 RETAINED			PART WORN NEW
Drawers, woollen long.	- Do - 1 - Do -			
Drawers, woollen short.	-	-		-
Drawers, cellular.	-			-
Drawers, cotton knitted.	-	-		-
Socks (Pairs).	1 (AMERICAN) 1 RETAINED			NEW
Gloves (Pairs	-			-
Shorts, khaki drill.	-	-		-
Shirts, khaki drill.	2 (AMERICAN) 2 LEFT BEHIND 16 MTHS			-

I hereby ~~agree~~ disagree that the assessed value of the items enumerated above may be recovered from the proceeds of my claim for compensation attached hereto. If the amount of compensation awarded is insufficient, I agree to the recovery of the balance

~~*(a) Paid by R.A.F. Allowances.~~

*(b) in cash.

Signature ....

Rank ...... F/LT ......

Personal No ...... 60572 ......

Prisoner of War No. ...... 3267 ......

Date ...... 18.5.45 ......

*Delete as necessary.

Distribution:- Air Ministry (P.6(a)) with Form 1784 attached if completed by the Officer.

APPENDIX 6

SGT CANTER'S
ESCAPE REPORT

MOST SECRET

M.I.9/S/P.G.(-) 1294

EVADED CAPTURE IN FRANCE.

The information contained in this report is to be treated as
MOST SECRET

STATEMENT BY

R.127907 Sgt. CANTER, Wilfred Lloyd, 408 Sqn. (R.C.A.F.) Bomber Command,R.A.F.

Left: GIBRALTAR, 23 Jun 43.   Arrived: LIVERPOOL, 29 Jun 43.

Date of Birth:	7 Feb 21.	Peacetime Profession: Salesman.
R.A.F.Service:	Since Aug 41.	Private Address: 252 Grace Street,
O.T.U.:	No. 23 (PERSHORE)	TORONTO, Ontario,
Post in crew:	Second pilot.	Canada.

1943

I was second pilot of a Halifax aircraft which took off from LEEMING BAR (Yorks) about 2200 hrs on 14 Apr 43 to bomb STUTTGART. On the return flight we were attacked by a night fighter over REIMS and the aircraft caught fire. The order to bale out was given about 0330 hrs, 15 Apr.

The only member of the crew whose name I know was P/O McKENZIE, R.A.A.F. (first pilot), who with the flight engineer was preparing to jump when I left the aircraft. The rear gunner, mid-upper gunner, and wireless operator jumped before me. About five hours later, while hiding at a deserted farm house, I saw a German patrol with two prisoners. I could not identify them, but they may have been the bomb aimer and navigator.

15 Apr
Baled out near REIMS

I came down about 0345 hrs just N.W. of REIMS. My leg was broken just above the ankle, and I was unable to walk. I gathered up my parachute and, after covering it with the harness, I started crawling in search of a hiding place, there being no cover in the field where I had come down. I crawled for about a mile, resting frequently. There were numerous Germans searching the district on foot, in cars, and on motor cycles, as several aircraft had come down that night. There was also a German barracks in the vicinity.

15 - 24 Apr
Sheltered in REIMS

Eventually I reached two small deserted farm houses, in one of which I hid after climbing in through a window. During the day I called to two women who approached the house. I speak a very little French, and I explained to them that I was R.A.F. and asked for help. In the late afternoon the women brought me food and clothing - I was wearing shoes, under my flying boots - and took away my uniform. In the evening their husbands escorted me by bicycle to the home of one of them in REIMS, where I was sheltered for nine days (15 - 24 Apr). I was then handed over to an organisation which arranged the rest of my journey.

INTERVIEWED BY: I.S.9(W) & O.R.S. Bomber Command.
30 Jun 43.

Distribution of this Report:
D.D.M.I.(P/W). M.I.9. I.S.9. I.S.9(X). I.S.9(W).
M.I.9(d). M.I.19. M.I.6 (for I.S.9(D)).
M.O.1(S.P.) (Lt.-Col. Butters). A.I.1(a) P/W.
W/Cdr. Harrison (A.L.O., M.I.9). Lt.-Col.Holt.
G.S."I", British Army Staff, Washington, for
POW Branch, MIS, War Dept (for COOK for JONES)
(2 copies)
C.I.O., H.Q: Bomber Command, R.A.F. (5 copies)
Fighter Command, R.A.F.
Coastal Command, R.A.F.

APPENDIX A - List of Helpers
Distribution: I.S.9. I.S.9(X).
M.I.6 (for I.S.9(D)). I.S.9(W).File.

APPENDIX B - Military Information
Distribution: A.I.1(a) P/W. M.I.10.
M.I.14. Bomber Command. M.I.19(2).
Lt.-Col. Holt. File.

APPENDIX C - Escape Information
Distribution: D.D.M.I.(P/W). I.S.9.
I.S.9(X). M.I.6 (for I.S.9(D)).
I.S.9(W). File.

APPENDIX D - Equipment & Training

APPENDIX 7

LONDON RESTAURANT RECOMMENTDATIONS

<u>Good London Restaurants</u> **83**

Pinoli's Wardour St (nr Leicester Square) lunch, dinner and Supper

Kempinski's Tavern - Swallow St (Regent Street) dinner, Supper dancing.

Martinez - " next door - Spanish food evening.

Trocadero - Shaftesbury Avenue - excellent teas (fruit)

S.F. Grill - Denman St (nr Regent Palace) all day - teas.

The Ivey - St Martin's Lane dinner.

Bristol Grill & Bar - Cork St W. (nr Bond St) dinner and dancing

St ? 's Hotel - Do - - Do - - do

Simons Hotel Brook St " "

Fischer's Rest. Clifford St. " " -

Aster Café Argyll St (opp Palladium) "

Savoy Grill Savoy Hotel Picadilly luncheon and Supper

Claridge's Causerie - Brook St. - Swedish hors d'oeuvre

Hog in the Pound - Davis St (Oxford St)

Mount Royal Marble Arch. Restaurant & Bar

Chicken Inn Haymarket. " & Snacks

Md. Tussaud's Rest.

I am the only running footman - Curzon St. Snacks & bars.

The New Paradise Regent St. Night Club

Landowne House Berkley Square Dinner

Th Chesrman 19th Century bars

Shepherds Shepherd's market - Mayfair - Dining.

Quaglinos's Jermyn St. W.1

Mirabelle Curzon St "

Prinins St James St. S.W. Fish only

Sheckeys Oyster Bar Wyndhams Court. Charing Cross Road Fish only

Le Coq. d'or Jermyn St.

84

Snow _____	Glasshouse St _ opp Reg Palace (Chinese Food)	
Cheshire Cheese	Fleet St _ _ Wednesday Special	
Gennaro	Southampton St. _ Risotto	
Rendezvous	Creek St (Soho) French all day	
Shearn	Tottenham Court Road _ Vegetarian _ Fruit Teas	
Scotts	Picadilly Circus	
Simpsons	Strand opp (Strand Palace Hotel)	
Leoni	_____ St _____	
Captains Cabin	Jermyn St !! Oxford St.	
Josef Picadilly	_____	
Coquille	_____ lane French seafood	
Turkish ___	_____ _ Turkish food.	
Spanish Club	Cavandish Sq	
(Service Flats	Stratford Court Oxford St.	

Lyric Mansions 22 Germain Tel Reg 2353
St James Court Buckingham Gate Vict 2360
Mount Royal Marble Arch £3·3·0 ex meals
Park West Edgware Rd. Do.
White House Albany Rd. Do.)

Snacks

____ the ____	Baker St _ Oxford ___	
Charley ____	____ Dock Rd	
The _____	Downshire Hill Hampstead (ideal on Sun)	
The Viking (Danish)	by Regal Palace	
Bee ____	Dean St good food	
Maxims	Grand St	
Quality ___	Leicester Sq	
Chef Victor	Wardour St	
Yorkshire Grey	Picadilly	

Moody's Irish House — Piccadilly House
Apple Tree — Bow St
Hole in the Wall. Theobalds Rd   Southampton Place
Dive —   Parliament St (Grill)
"Cl se Rest" Deman St.
Troika Rest" — Do —
Martins (Spanish) Ayr St (?)
Vanity Fair   Sackville St (good lunch)
Arts Club   Covent Garden
Price   Whitcomb St (Sandwiches only)
Cheese Shop   Jermyn St   off Piccadilly Arcade
Corlestins   Covent Garden
White Tower   Charlotte St
Josefs (Yugoslavian) Greek St.

APPENDIX 8

LONDON HOTEL RECOMMENDATIONS

86 _____ HOTELS

Almonds Hotel	Clifford St SW1
Barleys Hotel	Gloucester Rd S. Kensington
Berners Hotel	— do — — do —
Brent Bridge Hotel	
Browns Hotel	Dover St W1
Flemings Hotel	Jermyn St Piccadilly
Grosvenor Hotel	near Victoria Station
"	Duver St Oxford St smaller comfortable
Great Fosters	Egham Surrey (country club swimming etc)
Hotel Rembrandt	Cromwell Rd S. Kensington
Hotel Rubens	Buckingham Palace Rd
Hyde Park Hotel	Knightsbridge
Mayfair	Berkeley St
Park Lane Hotel	Green Park
Prooks Hotel	Dover St
Royal Court Hotel	Sloane Sq SW (good grill)
Selsdon Hotel	Croydon (NB on country club lines)
Bryanston Court Hotel	Bryanston St
Somerset Hotel	Orchard St SW
Symons Hotel	Brook St
Waldorf	Aldwych WC2
Cracker Club & Indian Club	Gerard St
New Yorker	Park Lane

HOTELS

Almonds Hotel	Clifford St, SW1
Baileys Hotel	Gloucester Road, S Kensington
Berners Hotel	Gloucester Road, S Kensington
Brent Bridge Hotel	
Browns Hotel	Dover Street, W1
Flemings Hotel	G….. Street, Piccadilly
Grosvenor Hotel	Near Victoria Station
Grosvenor Hotel	Davies St, Oxford Street, small & comfortable
Great Eastern	Egham Surrey (country club, swimming, etc)
Hotel Rembrandt	Cromwell Road, S Kensington
Hotel Rubens	Buckingham Palace Road
Hyde Park Hotel	Knightsbridge
Mayfair	Berkeley St
Park Lane Hotel	Green Park
Pratts Hotel	Dover Street
Royal Court Hotel	Sloane Square, SW (good grill)
Selsdon Park Hotel	Croydon (VG on country club lines)
Bryanston Court Hotel	Bryanston Street
Somerset Hotel	Orchard Street, SW
Symons Hotel	Brook Street
Waldorf	Aldwych WC2
Bracken Club & Tudor Club	Gerard Street
New Yorker	Park Lane

APPENDIX 9

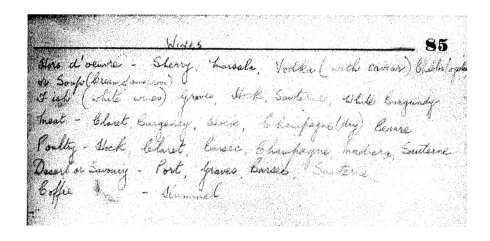

WINES

Hors d'Oeuves   - Sherry, Marsala, Vodka (with Caviar) …Chablis/Oysters..

or Soup (Cream of Mushroom)

Fish   (White wines) Graves, Hock, Sauterne, White Burgundy

Meat   - Claret, Burgundy, Hock, Champagne (day), Bearne

Poultry   - Hock, Claret, Barsec, Champagne,Madiera , Sauterne

Desert or Savoury   - Port, Graves, Barsec, Sauterne

Coffee   - Kummel

APPENDIX 10

SELECTION OF MENUS AND RECIPES

76 _Cooking Notes._

Casseroled steaks beaten cooked in butter & milk potatoes etc. seasoning to taste. Sweet sauces with meat e.g. pineapple with chicken - milk in soup. Potatoes & carrots in cakes.

Steak rolls   beat steak and boil till tender in deep fat. Drain & roll each steak in rolls with sage stuffing in centre, bake in hot oven

Spam Virginia Pie   Two tins spam, 2 cups bread crumbs, 2 tbls cream, Chop spam & mix into firm dough & make flat cakes. Sprinkle both sides with sugar. Fry & bake in oven with honey & margarine on top. Serve with fried potatoes.

Blood Sausage   mix chopped sausage with 1½ tins paté salt, onions, 2 tbls margarine ½ cup skim or cream cheese - bake in oven

Fruit Shortcake   3 cups biscuit crumbs, 2 teaspoons salt. Work in 3 tbls creamed butter & 1 cup milk till soft dough. Roll out to ½ thickness. Cut into rounds & bake in flat pan for 15 mins. Mash 3 cups fruit or sugar split biscuits & butter each half & bake again. Jam spread between & on top. Serve with thick cream.

Peanut Shortcake   3 cups bread or biscuit crumbs 2 tbls salt, 1-2 tbls butter. 3 - 4 tbl peanut butter, 3 tbl sugar. Knead with little milk. Roll ½ thick, cut into fingers, decorate with split peanuts, bake 16 mins

Kriegie Syrup Pudding ¾ cup burnt sugar, ½ cup butter ½ cup sour milk ½ cup treacle or honey, 1 cup boiled barley mix together and add dry mixture of 2 cups biscuit & bread crumbs ¾ cups raisins. Bake covered in slow oven then spread with marg and thick syrup to brown in hot oven

Strawberry Shortcake   mix 2½ tbl baking powder with 3 cups flour & 2 tsps salt and work in 3 tbls soft butter, work in cup or more of milk till soft dough. Pat out to ½" thickness on floured board. Cut out biscuits and bake in greased pan for 16 mins. Mash up 2 lbs fruit with sugar till sweet. Split biscuits when done put butter inside and on top. Serve with cream - Works with all fruit

Kriegie chocolate Pudding   canadian biscuits broken finely, milk, butter, cocoa sugar (raisins if desired) Served hot or cold.

Chinese Cooking

Vegs usually chopped & fried in lard, oil or butter (very little) for 3-5 mins then cooked in frying pan by addition of water

Meat, veg & seasoning served mixed

Seasoning to develop taste uses salt, vinegar, soya, bean sauce, sugar etc to eliminate odour etc, sherry, ginger, spring onions, garlic

Serving (1) Cold dishes (2) Fried dishes and wine (3) Braised and stewed dishes with rice (4) Veg dishes or soup (6) Sweet

Egg Soup beat 2 eggs in basin boil 1 pint stock and add 1 tbls lard or oil 1 tbls soya bean sauce pour over beaten egg & stir gently Serve when egg cooked

Boiling rice Cover rice with water Pour rice into thickness of ½" into saucepan or iron pot Cover pan until water nearly all absorbed. Then simmer on low heat for 20 mins covered to prevent burning. If veg or meat is to be added, add on top of rice for final 20 minutes In 1st stage butter lard oil or salt can be added

Fry porridge, pastry patties in deep fat

Ceylon Curry plate of fried rice- rice in centre. Around rice on plate grated or baked nuts, raisins, fried potatoes in slices & curried dishes ie 1. c chicken 2. c fish 3. c 4. 5 vegs. 4. Coconut grated 6. Cucumber soaked in vinegar salt pepper 6. c tomatoes 7. fried curried onions 1. 2. 3. 6. 7. curried 1267 chopped or sliced. 3. also bananas fried & fried in deep fat chopped Fried egg on top of all or sliced omelette

To Squadron (R.A.F.) dates mix in double boiler 3 cups chopped dates, 1 cup chopped walnuts ½ cup chopped almonds, 1 tbls root ginger, 1 tbls butter, serve hot with whipped cream.

Coffee cream mould cream 2oz butter + 2 tbls sugar in warm bowl add 1 beaten egg, 4 tbls milk, 3 tbls conc. coffee, with cake or biscuit crumbs enough to thicken mixture. Beat fiercely in warm place till smooth. Wet a mould and pour in mixture Serve when set

Beetroot slices. (Savoury) slice boiled beet ½" thick rounds, dip in thick batter or thick cornflour paste Sprinkle with grated cheese and fry quickly in butter.

French fried Shrimps Shell shrimps dip in egg mixture roll in biscuit bread or in crushed cereal and fry in deep hot fat until brown

Ice Cream Crush fruit - fresh strawberries and syrup (sugar water boiled) freeze mixture, cut in slices and serve with ice cream

French Toast Bread butter and jam sandwich dipped in batter and fried serve hot with whipped cream

Egg tomato & bacon - Brown chopped bacon and onions in butter add fresh tomatoes at first stage. Add salt and seasoning. Cook slowly. Add half small can of egg tomato ketchup or juice. Allow to cook until mixture starts to thicken. Add eggs whole, Cover pan and cook until eggs are done

Pineapple syrup cake - make syrup out of butter and brown sugar. Place pineapple cubes in baking dish. Mix a batter of eggs and flour and add syrup mixture to sweeten batter, Pour over pineapple and bake in hot oven. Serve hot with cream

Dried porridge allow very thick and well salted porridge to cool. Drop 1 tb of porridge at a time into a very hot frying pan with a little butter. Turn don't baste and brown surface crisp. Serve immediately with honey, syrup or sugar, surrounded with banana slices (or other fruit) and lots of thick cream.

Dice lightly boiled potatoes mix with chopped onions beaten eggs. Fry in butter

Corn on the cob boil water add salt and cobs and boil until done. Smear with butter salt and pepper and eat from cob

Ham and pineapple Takes thick slices of ham and fry on one sides until brown. Turn ham & put pineapple ring with marshmallow in centre on slice until other side is brown Serve on toast with fried bread.

Breakfast fry pineapple rings in egg batter and serve with sausage, bacons and tomato. Pancakes with egg and bacon.

Sandwich peanut butter and banana sliced between new white bread baked or toasted first.

Shredded Wheat Takes wheat and dip in hot water fry in buttered pans with pat of butter on top. Fry covered until bottom is brown, Serve in hot porridge or with hot milk and fruit

Cheese sandwiches and bacon Toast on one side two slices of bread, butter untoasted sides and put slices of cheese on top. Spread with mustard and cover with chopped bacon and bake in oven until crisp (bacon) make sandwich

Egg and Spinach Wash ¼ lb spinach and fry in a little butter for 3 mins Chop spinach very fine and beat with 3 eggs & ½ tsp salt, fry for 3 minutes until green & creamy

Cold potato salad stir into creamed, mashed potatoes, chopped onion & chopped hard boiled eggs.

APPENDIX 11

RED CROSS PARCELS

Due to the combined efforts of the British Canadian ... as worked with one relief cross parcel per week which ... prisoner of war camp partly compatible as far ... The contents are as follows:

Red Cross Parcels

British

MEAT & VEG	1 Tin
MEAT ROLL	1 Tin
BISCUITS	1 Tin
CHEESE	2 oz
CONDENSED MILK	1 Tin
SUGAR	4 oz
MARGARINE	3 oz
JAM	3 oz
SALMON	1 Tin
TEA	2 oz
COCOA	4 oz
CHOCOLATE	4 oz
SOAP	1 BAR

Canadian

CORNED BEEF	1 Tin
SPAM	1 Tin
BISCUITS	1 Box
CHEESE	11 oz
POWDERED MILK	1 Tin
SUGAR	7 oz
BUTTER	1 LB
JAM	1 LB
SALMON	1 Tin
COFFEE	6 oz
PRUNES	3 oz
CHOCOLATE	5 oz
SOAP	1 BAR
SARDINES	1 Tin
SALT	1 Packet
RAISINS	7 oz

American

CORNED BEEF	1 Tin
SPAM	1 Tin
BISCUITS	1 Box
CHEESE	8 oz
POWDERED MILK	1 Tin
SUGAR	8 oz
MARGARINE	1 LB
JAM	6 oz
SALMON	1 Tin
NESCAFE	1 Tin
PRUNES	1 LB
CHOCOLATE	4 oz
SOAP	2 BARS
SARDINES	1 Tin
MEAT PASTE	1 Tin
ORANGE CRYSTALS	2 PACKETS
CIGARETTES	80

N. Zealand

CORNED BEEF	1 Tin
TONGUE	1 Tin
DRIED PEAS	2 oz
CHEESE	8 oz
CONDENSED MILK	1 Tin
SUGAR	8 oz
BUTTER	1 LB
JAM	1 LB
CAFE AU LAIT	1 Tin
TEA	4 oz
CIGARETTES	50
CHOCOLATE	4 oz

APPENDIX 12   BOOKS READ

See how they run	Jerrard Tickell
Home Match	A Bennett
Sea Hawk	R Sabatini
	Stella Benson
The Harsh Voice	Rebecca West
… All Hands	H T Templeton
Prelude to Christopher	Eleanor Dare
Mystery of the Creek	J J Faryeon
Yellow Peril	J J Faryeon
After the Verdict	R Hichens
Honourable Jim	Baroness Orgzy
My Antonia	Willa Cather
Sacred & Profane Love	Arnold Bennett
Morning Tide	Neil M Gunn
Nicolette	Baroness Orgzy
Woman with the Fan	Robert Hichens
Blue Eyes and Grey	Baroness Onezy
Gallows Grange	Henry Holt
Murderers Luck	Henry Holt
Elsie and the Child	Arnold Bennett
The Cask	Freeman W Croft
The Old Curiosity Shop	C Dickens
Slade	Warwick Deeping
Jungle Ways	
Unsere Wehrmacht……	
Mantrap	Sinclair Lewis
A Mans Man	Ian Hay

A Knight on Wheels	Ian Hay
The Little Ladyship	Ian Hay
Table Talk	William Hazlett
The General goes to Far…..	A J Cronin…..
Sorrell & son	Warwick Deeping
Dr Jekyll & Mr Hyde	Robert Lewis Stevenson
Kidnapped	Robert Lewis Stevenson
Desmond Rourke - Irishman	John Haslette
Hurricane (the)	Lordhoff and Hall
Happy go Lucky	Ian Hay
The Happy Returns	C S Forester
The unpractised Heart	L A G Strong
Prestor John	John Buchan
The case of the Velvet Claws	Erle Stanley Gardner
Lost Horizon	James Hilton
The Riddle of the Sands	Erkine Childers
Trents Last Case	E C Bentley
Africa Calling	Roger Courtney
The Flight of the Heron	D K Broster
The Gleam in the North	D K Broster
Wind in the Willows	K Graham
Quest of the Griffins	R Atkinson
The Gentleman of the Party	A G Street
Greenery Street	D McKail
Gone with the Wind	Margaret Mitchell
Hornblower R N	Forester
One Good Turn	Valentines
Rebecca	Daphne de Maurier

Straws into Gold	Edmund Vale
Fire Over England	A E W Mason
Honeymark	A E W Mason
Cold Comfort Farm	Stella Gibbons
Buttercups and Daisies	Compton Mackenzies
Tom Sawyer	Mark Twain
Gullivers Travels	J Swift
Musk and Amber	A E W Mason
Flowering Wilderness	John Goldsworthy
The Silver Spoon	John Goldsworthy
Across the river	John Goldsworthy
Broadsides	R W Daly
Beau	P C Wren
Beau Geste	P C Wren
Beau Ideals	P C Wren
Laughing Gas	P G Wodehouse
Modern Comedy	John Goldsworthy
Along the Road	A Huxby
Maid in Waiting	John Goldsworthy
Passing the 3rd floor back	C Houghton
Diversity of Creatures	R Kipling
The White Company	A C Doyle
John Cornelius	Hugh Walpole
Detective Ben	J J Faryeon
Valiant Dust	J J Faryeon
Sanctuary Island	E Wallace
The Green Puck	E Wallace
Black Mischief	Evelyn Waugh

The Red House Mystery	A A Milne
Three Just Men	E Wallace
Such Power is Dangerous	D Wheatley
Story of San Michele	Axel Munthe
Pipe	Ian Hay
Goodbye Mr Chips	J Hilton
Our Mr Wrenn	Sinclair Lewis
Full House	M J Farrell
Ask for Mercy	Barry Perowne
Peters Mother	Lady Clifford
Verners Pride	Mrs H Wood
Cast Lynn	Mrs H Wood
Wassmuss	Chris Sykes
Fortnight in September	R C Sherrif
Figure of Light	C Mackenzie
Memories and Vagaries	Axel Munthe
The Common Glory	David Pilgrims
The Gantillons	Robert Liddel
The Irish Sketch Book	W N Thackeray
The Scarlet Letter	N Hawthorne
The Wages of Virtue	P C Wrenn
Franz Schubert	
Chesterfields letters to his son	Lord Chesterfield
Autobiography of a super Tramp	W H Davis
And then there were none	

APPENDIX   13

PLAYS - SHOWS - BELARIA

27 March 1944	Rope	Patrick Hamilton
2 May 1944	Hay Fever	Noel Coward
24 May 1944	Arsenic & Old Lace	Noel Coward
12 June 1944	Give us the Air	J Hill & R Ryder
19 June 1944	We Were Dancing	Noel Coward
21 June 1944	In the Zone	
22 June 1944		Noel Coward
28 August 1944	Someone at the Door	D Christie & Jas Nordhoff
3 October 1944	French Without Tears	Terence Rattigan
29 March 1944	Band Show	Station Band
21 July 1944	Band Show (Open Air)	Station Band
14 August 1944	Film Show - Dixie Duggan	
11 September 1944	Band Show	Station Band
21 October 1944	"Major Barbara" (Radio Play)	
	The Astonished Ostrich	
	George and Margaret	
	Mr Corn Comes to Town	
	The 1st Mrs Fraser	
	Fanfare	
	Tony Draws a Horse	

APPENDIX   14

VIPS FLOWN

General McCreery

Lady McCreery

General Winterton

Dr.Figl (Austrian Chancellor)

Lt General Nott-Bower

General Steele

Lady Steele

Sir Henry Mack (Ambassador)

Lady Mack

Sir Arthur Street

Mr Hynd (Duchy of Lancaster)

Lt. General Packard

Field Marshall Deverill

General Adams

Air Vice Marshall Storer

Sir Gilmore Jenkins

Lady Winterton

Mr De Freites

HC Spaight (AOC CMF)

Air Vice Marshall Statton (AOC 46 GP)

Lord Packenham

Mr J Jones MP

Provost Marshall of the RAF

General Bolte (USA)

Air Marshall Sir Brian Baker (C in C Transport Command))

Marshall of the RAF - Lord Tedder

Lady Tedder

Rt.Hon Mr A Henderson

Viscount Montgomery

Princess Margaret

Margot Fonteyn

Pamela May

Lord Schuster

General Weir

BIBLIOGRAPHY

W A McIlroy	POW Scrap Book, Flying Records, Family Correspondence.
MacKenzie Family	Family Records, Letters, Notes, Photographs
Bill Lott	Letters and Notes
Alex Ager	Letters and Diary Notes
Barbara Tracy	POW Records, Flying Log of Don Belyea (her Grandfather)
Philippe Gravez	Notes, Records, Photographs
Eric Hebert	Notes, Records, Photographs
Don Charlwood	No Moon Tonight Goodall Publishing, 2000
BA James	Moonless Night Leo Cooper, 2004
WR Chorley	Bomber Command Losses, 1943 & 1944 Midland Publishing, 2005
Norman LR Franks	Fighter Command Losses, 1942 & 1943 Midland Publishing, 1998
Dudley Saward	Bomber Harris Sphere Books, 1986
Albert Speer	Inside the Third Reich Phoenix Paperbacks, 1995
John Nichol & Tony Rennell	The Last Escape Penguin Books, 2003
Anthony Beevor	Berlin. The Downfall, 1945 Penguin Books, 2003
Alan Cooper	Air Battle of the Ruhr Airlife Publishing, 2000
James Taylor & Martin Davidson	Bomber Crew Hodder & Stoughton, 2005
Sir Winston Churchill	My Early Life Fontana Books, 1971
Airey Neave	Saturday at M.I.9 Grafton Books, 1989

158

Patrick Wilson	The War Behind the Wire Leo Cooper, 2000
Bryce Coussens	The Log: Sagan Bryce Coussens, 1947
Eric Brown	Wings on My Sleeves Weidenfeld & Nicholson, 2006
Geoffrey Brooks	Hitler's Terror Weapons Leo Cooper, 2002
Delve & Jacobs	The Six Year Offensive Cassel Imprint, 1992
Public Records Office, Kew	Various Records/Documents